Hebrews Study Guide

To Susannah & Ben

With much love from Grandy

x

Hebrews Study Guide

John Morris

The Christadelphian
404 Shaftmoor Lane, Hall Green, Birmingham B28 8SZ, UK

2020

First published 2020

© 2020 The Christadelphian Magazine and Publishing Association

ISBN 978 0 85189 433 1 (print edition)
ISBN 978 0 85189 434 8 (electronic edition)

Printed and bound in the UK by
CMP (UK) Limited

Contents

What is a Study Guide?

1. Aims: The overriding aim of all Bible study is that through knowledge and understanding of the word of God a person may become "wise unto salvation through faith which is in Christ Jesus" (2 Timothy 3:15, KJV).

   "Study Guides" are designed to explain the straightforward teachings of scripture and where appropriate to emphasise:

   a. First principles of doctrine

   b. Practical outcomes

   They should be helpful to young people, to those who are "young in the faith", who often have very little background knowledge of the scriptures, and to those of all ages and experience who enjoy straightforward, uncomplicated study of the Bible.

2. Other features of Study Guides

   a. Layout: After a brief introduction to the book, essential background information is provided before looking at the text in more detail. Headings and verse references make it easy to use the guide for looking up information on any section of the Bible text.

   b. Bible versions: This Guide mainly uses the New King James Version as a basis, as this helps to overcome problems of archaic expressions that exist in the Authorised (King James) Version (AV / KJV), which remains the most used translation in Christadelphian ecclesias today. Other versions can sometimes assist in clarifying a particular passage, but some popular modern versions are unreliable and betray the doctrinal bias of their translators.

   c. Manageable sections: Each Guide is divided into units of study which are not too long. This will make it easier for individuals or groups to make progress. An hour's concentrated and productive study on a regular basis is likely to yield good results.

   d. Visual help: The prophets and the Lord Jesus himself used visual illustrations to communicate their message. While the prime emphasis is on the written word, visual help is given wherever possible to increase understanding.

   e. Use alongside the Bible: The student must have a Bible open alongside the Guide. It is recommended at the outset that important information is marked in the Bible. Have a pencil at the ready.

   f. Points to ponder: Each chapter concludes with thoughts for reflection and topics to encourage further study.

   g. Prayer: We are studying the word of God. Before commencing any Bible study we must ask God's blessing on our activity. Thank God for making the Bible available to us, so that through it we may come to know Him and to look forward to His coming kingdom.

Here is a prayer that sums up our aim:

"Open thou mine eyes, that I may behold wondrous things out of thy law."

(Psalm 119:18, KJV)

Preface

One way of appreciating a book of the Bible is to reflect on what we would miss if we did not have it. In relation to the Letter to the Hebrews, this is a sombre thought. Without Hebrews, there would be:

- No New Testament reference to the enigmatic figure of Melchizedek;

- No examination of the significance of the tabernacle;

- No detailed exposition of the high priesthood of the Lord Jesus;

- No review of men and women of faith who lived as strangers and pilgrims on the earth;

- No specific exhortation to "go forth to him, outside the camp, bearing his reproach".

How grateful we should be that, by God's grace, this Letter has been written and preserved!

THE Letter to the Hebrews is a masterly exposition of the work of the Lord Jesus Christ as Mediator and High Priest through whom the believer can now "enter the holiest". Jesus – better than the angels, better than Moses, Aaron or Joshua, by a better covenant – has done what the Law of Moses could never achieve, reconciling us to God.

Every disciple is keen to know who the writer was, who the original readers were, their circumstances, the date of the Letter etc. We cannot answer these questions with total certainty, and in the end it does not matter. God has decided what we should know, and we are given enough to be able to understand the wonderful truths about God's purpose in His Son that are expounded in this Letter.

Hebrews was, of course, first addressed to Jews – Jews brought up under the Law of Moses and now, as believers in Christ, caught between their loyalty to that Law and their new commitment to the Gospel. Readers of the Letter today are in a very different situation. Is Hebrews, then, at all relevant to Gentile disciples two thousand years away from the generation who first read these words? The Letter is timeless: it teaches what every disciple needs to know, that is, how the types and shadows of the Law of Israel pointed forward to the coming of God's Son, his death and exaltation to the Father's right hand. It teaches that we must resist the pull of the world and go forth in faith, bearing his reproach.

Paul (who we believe to be the writer) does not spare his readers; he digs deep, and we must be prepared to delve deeply ourselves. This Study Guide is a little longer than some, as there is so much to examine – and still not every detail is covered. At the end of each chapter, there are 'Points to Ponder': questions or thoughts arising from the text that may help the reader to reflect on the teaching of the Letter. With serious effort and prayer, the rich beauties of this unique part of God's word will be revealed.

John Morris
Birmingham, UK, 2020

Hebrews in a hundred words

GOD who spoke to the fathers has now spoken through His Son Jesus, the Mediator of a new and better covenant. By his death our sins are purged, and it is time to let go of our devotion to the temple and the Law. What the High Priest did on the Day of Atonement each year, Christ – an eternal High Priest of the order of Melchizedek – has done once for all. He has entered the Holiest with his own blood, and we can have boldness to enter God's presence through faith in him. "Let us go forth ... bearing his reproach."

"John's record is to the [other] gospels what the letter to the Hebrews is to the other epistles." – John Carter, A Postscript on the Symbolic Language in the Gospel of John, in *Parables of the Messiah*

Introduction

THE AUTHOR AND HIS READERS

HEBREWS is an anonymous letter. From an early date, it bore the title "To Hebrews", but no author's name. It is not essential to know who the writer was: perhaps the Letter is left anonymous to emphasise the simple fact that God was the Author. God in any case ensured that the Letter was accepted by faithful believers as part of inspired scripture, though in the wider 'church' there were, for some time, doubts whether this book should be included in the New Testament canon.

The first recipients of the Letter knew who sent it: that much is clear from the author's acknowledgement of the readers' kindness to him (10:34), his desire to see them again soon, with Timothy (13:19,23), and other personal comments.

Authorship

For many centuries, Paul's name was associated with Hebrews, and his name is inserted in the title of the Letter in early English versions, including Tyndale and the Authorised / King James Version. The view of most modern scholars seems to be that, whoever wrote Hebrews, it was **not** Paul – though no convincing case is made for another author.

Who else might have written Hebrews? Luke is a possibility: a number of key words and phrases in Hebrews echo the language found in Luke's Gospel and Acts. Barnabas has been suggested: he was a Levite well acquainted with the Law and with life in Jerusalem. Apollos was "born at Alexandria, an eloquent man and mighty in the Scriptures" (Acts 18:24) and it is claimed that this epistle has traces of the style of someone from Alexandria in Egypt. And we still have not exhausted all the suggestions that have been made about authorship. In addition, there is an ancient opinion that Paul wrote an original letter in *Hebrew* for those in Jerusalem, and that Luke then produced a version of the letter in his own polished *Greek* to be sent to Greek-speaking ecclesias – and that **this** is the one we now have in our hands. A variant of this suggestion is that Paul dictated the letter, in Greek, to Luke who then included characteristic words and phrases of his own.

Without seeking to be dogmatic on the issue, we shall assemble evidence that has convinced many that **Paul** was indeed the author of Hebrews. Until his experience on the Damascus road, Saul the Pharisee had "been exceedingly zealous for the traditions of my fathers" (Galatians 1:14; note also Acts 22:3; 26:5). He

The first page of Hebrews in Tyndale's version: from a facsimile of a 1525 / 1526 edition

had experienced the same heart-searchings as those to whom this Letter is addressed. And although we rightly think of Paul as the apostle to the Gentiles, we should not forget what the Lord said to Ananias: "He is a chosen vessel of mine to bear my name before Gentiles, kings, **and the children of Israel**" (Acts 9:15). Paul did have a commission to Jews as well as Gentiles.

If you had to choose a writer who could deal sympathetically with the Hebrews' problems, surely it would be Paul? He knew all too well the mindset of those (they doubtless included former friends and colleagues) who were trying to cling on to the Law.

Arguments for and against Paul

"Hebrews", as a term referring to Abraham's race, is a rare word in the New Testament. Two mentions out of a total of three (the other is in Acts 6:1) are from the pen of Paul:

"Are they **Hebrews**? So am I. Are they Israelites? So am I. Are they the seed of Abraham? So am I." (2 Corinthians 11:22)

"If anyone else thinks he may have confidence in the flesh, I more so: circumcised the eighth day, of the stock of Israel, of the tribe of Benjamin, a Hebrew of the **Hebrews**." (Philippians 3:5)

It is not quite a proof of authorship, but "Hebrews" is a word we can certainly associate with Paul.

Those who argue against Paul often quote a verse which speaks of "so great a salvation, which at the first began to be spoken by the Lord, and was **confirmed unto us by those who heard him**" (2:3). From this you might conclude that the writer was a **second** generation believer who had not heard Jesus preach, whereas Paul claims a **first-hand** revelation:

"Have not I seen Jesus Christ our Lord?" (1 Corinthians 9:1; 15:8)

"I neither received [the gospel] from man, nor was I taught it, but it came through the revelation of Jesus Christ." (Galatians 1:12)

But there need be no contradiction: in Hebrews 2:3 Paul could simply be saying that, thirty or more years previously, the first disciples were taught by the Lord, and meanwhile others like himself and his readers had the Gospel confirmed to them.

Scholars say that the style of Hebrews is unique; it is written, apparently, in a smoother, more elegant Greek than the thirteen letters that we attribute with certainty to Paul. But this difference can be explained: those thirteen letters are all addressed to ecclesias in the Roman world, ecclesias with a large **Gentile** membership. Paul's style of writing, his way of reasoning, will naturally be different when he writes – as a "Hebrew of the Hebrews" – to an exclusively **Jewish** readership. How one writes a letter depends on who the recipient is: we write a letter to an old school-friend in one style, but to a new acquaintance in a very different style.

The following words of Paul are surely significant in this context:

PAUL'S LOVE FOR HIS FELLOW-COUNTRYMEN

"I have great sorrow and continual grief in my heart. For I could wish that I myself were accursed from Christ for my brethren, my countrymen according to the flesh" (Romans 9:2,3).

"To the Jews I became as a Jew, that I might win the Jews; **to those who are under the law, as under the law**, that I might win those who are under the law ... I have become all things to all men, that I might by all means save some." (1 Corinthians 9:20-22)

Paul, in other words, consciously adapted his style to his audience. Those words from Corinthians are of course especially apt, because the primary object of this Letter to the Hebrews was to "win those who are under the law".

In what language was Hebrews written?

The Letter has come down to us in Greek, but was there perhaps a Hebrew (Aramaic) original? Paul **understood** Hebrew (Acts 26:14), **spoke** Hebrew (Acts 21:40; 22:2), and was without doubt capable of **writing** Hebrew. Commentators say on linguistic evidence, however, that the original Letter must have been in Greek:

> "It is impossible to imagine any Aramaic phrase which could have suggested to a translator the opening clause of the epistle ... and similar difficulties offer themselves throughout the book in the free and masterly use of compound words which have no Aramaic equivalents" (B. F. Westcott, *The Epistle to the Hebrews*).

We might add that Paul would surely want his Letter to be understood by Greek-speaking

TYPICAL WORDS AND PHRASES IN PAUL'S LETTERS

If Paul wrote Hebrews, then you might expect to find words, idioms and metaphors in this Letter that are also found in other Letters of Paul, and in the speeches of Paul in the Acts. Here are just four of many examples:

1. **"With his own blood"** (the expression occurs only in the following places):
   - Acts 20:28 (from Paul's farewell to the elders of Ephesus) – "... which he purchased **with his own blood**".
   - Hebrews 9:12 – "... **with his own blood** he entered the Most Holy Place".
   - Hebrews 13:12 – "... that he might sanctify the people **with his own blood**".

2. **"To destroy death"** (only in Paul's epistles – and Hebrews):
   - 1 Corinthians 15:26 – "The last enemy that will be **destroyed** is **death**".
   - 2 Timothy 1:10 – "Jesus Christ, who has **abolished** [destroyed] **death**".
   - Hebrews 2:14 – "... that through death he might **destroy** him who had the power of **death**".

3. **"Carried about"** (a nautical metaphor):
   - Ephesians 4:14 – "... that we should no longer be ... **carried about** with every wind of doctrine".
   - Hebrews 13:9 – "Do not be **carried about** with various and strange doctrines".

4. **"I am confident [persuaded] concerning you"**:
   - Romans 15:14 – "I myself am **confident** concerning **you**, my brethren".
   - 2 Thessalonians 3:4 – "And we have **confidence** in the Lord concerning **you**".
   - Philemon :21 – "Having **confidence** in **your** obedience, I write to you".
   - Hebrews 6:9 – "But, beloved, we are **confident** of better things concerning **you**".

At a number of places throughout this Study Guide, parallel verses from other letters which 'echo' a particular Hebrews passage are quoted in the inner column alongside.

believers too, initially in Jerusalem but also (in due course) elsewhere.

This last point connects with something that the Apostle Peter wrote: Peter refers to a letter which "our beloved brother **Paul**, according to the wisdom given to him, **has written to you** [Jewish Christians in the diaspora], as also in all his epistles ... in which are some things hard to understand" (2 Peter 3:15,16). No other letter of Paul fits this description, so the Letter to Hebrews (written in Greek) could very well be the one to which Peter refers. And if not, where is that letter?

Notice, too, that according to Peter this letter to Jewish Christians can be classed as "Scripture", for he adds in verse 16: "unstable people twist [Paul's epistles] to their own destruction, as they do also the rest of the Scriptures".

But, having made the point that Paul's thirteen Letters show similarities with Hebrews, we must not be surprised to discover that there are also big **differences** between these letters. Though by the same author, they were written to very different audiences, with very different problems, and using different vocabulary. For example, in Hebrews the work of the Lord Jesus is described in terms of his high priesthood and his fulfilment of the Law, whereas in Romans we have the language of justification, righteousness and grace. Romans was for a mixed readership of Jews and Gentiles in the diaspora (the Jewish world outside Palestine); Hebrews was for a Jewish readership close to the temple.

Every letter of the New Testament is different, depending on the writer and the situation of the readers. Note the comment alongside: though relating to the Pastoral Epistles, the general point being made here is that care must be exercised when drawing conclusions about authorship merely from vocabulary and style.

Many commentators agree that Hebrews contains echoes of Stephen's speech (Acts 7). That is easily explained if Paul wrote Hebrews,

"The language of the Letters to Timothy and Titus differs in many respects from all other in the New Testament, not least in the unusual vocabulary used by Paul. The fact that between 146 and 188 words in these letters occur nowhere else in the New Testament ... has been used as an argument against their authenticity" (Alfred Nicholls, *Letters to Timothy and Titus*, pages 5,6).

PAUL'S 'SIGNATURE'

The closing blessing of Hebrews is "Grace be with you all" (13:25). Compare this with the corresponding 'signature' phrases in other letters of Paul:

- "The grace of our Lord Jesus Christ be with you all" (Romans 16:24; Philippians 4:23; 2 Thessalonians 3:18).

- "The grace of our Lord Jesus Christ be with you" (1 Corinthians 16:23; 1 Thessalonians 5:28).

- "The grace of the Lord Jesus Christ, and the love of God, and the communion of the Holy Spirit be with you all" (2 Corinthians 13:14).

- "The grace of our Lord Jesus Christ be with your spirit" (Galatians 6:18; Philemon :25).

- "Grace be with all those who love our Lord Jesus Christ in sincerity" (Ephesians 6:24).

- "Grace be with you" (Colossians 4:18; 1 Timothy 6:21; 2 Timothy 4:22).

- "Grace be with you all" (Titus 3:15).

The similarity between these blessings and the one at the end of Hebrews surely tells us something. The endings of the letters of James, Peter, John and Jude are unlike any of the above.

for he was there, but not so readily explained if the author was someone else.

Who were the recipients?

This is a letter addressed to a particular ecclesia – not to the whole of that ecclesia but to a section of its membership. In the final chapter there are no fewer than three mentions of "those who rule over you" (13:7,17,24), making a distinction between a particular group of members and their elders, and hinting that the readers had not been diligent in following the example and instruction of those rulers.

It was an ecclesia with which the writer was familiar, and he hopes to visit them again shortly: "I especially urge you to do this, that I may be restored to you the sooner" (13:19).

Where, then, was this ecclesia? There have been as many suggestions about the location of the readers as there have been about the writer. Were they Jewish believers in Rome? Alexandria? Asia Minor? Jerusalem? The answer has to be **Jerusalem**. It is a good practice, before we read any New Testament epistle, to look for relevant background information in the Acts of the Apostles: by reading the accounts of the establishment of an ecclesia like that at Corinth, for example, we are better able to understand the epistles to Corinth. So much in Acts seems to point to Jerusalem as the ecclesia to which a letter to Hebrews is likely to have been sent. In the following chapter some of this detailed

evidence is brought together, but in addition there are the following points.

The Jerusalem ecclesial membership would have been overwhelmingly Jewish (including the Hellenists, or Grecian Jews mentioned in Acts 6:1). "Hebrews" seems an appropriate name for such a congregation. In fact, following on from Paul's usage of the word "Hebrews", referred to above, it seems that this term is particularly reserved for those of purest Jewish descent, whereas "Jews" or "Israelites" are more general, everyday terms for the descendants of Abraham, Isaac and Jacob. The Jews of Jerusalem would definitely consider themselves to be Jews of the purest descent and the strictest in upholding the Jewish faith. There could even be a tinge of irony in the title of the letter. The heading, "To Hebrews", may have been intended as a challenge to those who were still boasting of their ancestry and taking pride in the temple and the Law.

If Jerusalem was **not** the destination of this Letter, then there is no New Testament letter to the ecclesia in Jerusalem. Would that not appear strange?

The time and place of writing

Many years had passed since the ascension of Jesus. It seems unlikely that James the Lord's brother was still alive: if he was, surely he would have had sufficient authority to deal with the Hebrews' problem without calling for outside help. James was martyred around AD 62. If Paul is the writer, then Hebrews has to be written before AD 68 (the approximate date of his death). Earlier in this chapter we mentioned Peter's (probable) reference to Hebrews in 2 Peter 3:15,16. If Hebrews is in fact the epistle Peter had in mind, then of course 2 Peter must have been written **after** Hebrews: a suggested date for 2 Peter is AD 65.

By AD 66 the Jewish War had begun, bringing turmoil to life in Jerusalem, with its climax in AD 70. The saints could "see the Day approaching" (10:25). There is no direct mention of the destruction of Jerusalem (an event which, had it already happened, would surely have been referred to), yet it is hinted at: "Here we have no continuing city, but we seek the one to come" (13:14). Dark clouds were gathering, Roman armies would soon destroy the beloved city, and then the temple and everything associated with it would be no more. As far as the Letter to the Hebrews is concerned, however, the catastrophe of AD 70 has not yet come.

Taking all this into account, we suggest a 'window' of writing **between AD 62-64**.

Where was the writer? The words "those from Italy greet you" (13:24) may suggest that the writer was in **Rome**. Paul was released from his first Roman imprisonment in approximately AD 62, so he could well have written the Letter during his subsequent period of freedom.

An alternative suggestion is that Paul wrote Hebrews in AD 57-59, while in prison in Caesarea, and before the journey to Rome. In that event, "those from Italy" would be brothers and sisters travelling **from** Italy and passing through Caesarea.

We shall return to the circumstances surrounding the writing of Hebrews in the chapter headed "The problem" (see page 13).

Is Hebrews a Letter?

This may seem an odd question to be asking, but commentators point out that Hebrews lacks many features of a letter, particularly at the beginning. It is really more of a thesis or dissertation. On the other hand, a thesis is not usually punctuated by exhortations, as is Hebrews. The writer himself considers the Letter to be primarily an exhortation, appealing to his readers to "bear with the word of exhortation, for I have written to you in few words" (13:22). There are echoes in Hebrews of Paul's speech in the synagogue at Antioch in Pisidia, also described as a "word of exhortation" (Acts 13:15) – a homily based on the readings for the day. For us, Hebrews is compelling both as a dissertation and as an exhortation.

AD 30
Ascension of Jesus

AD 36
Paul's first visit to Jerusalem

AD 43
Death of James (John's brother)

AD 49
Jerusalem Council

AD 57
Paul's meeting with James; arrest and trials

AD 65
?Death of Peter

AD 68
Death of Paul

AD 33
Death of Stephen / Conversion of Saul

AD 46
Paul's second visit to Jerusalem

AD 62
Death of James (Jesus' brother)

AD 66
Jewish uprising against Rome

AD 70
Fall of Jerusalem

AD 47-48
First Missionary Journey

AD 53-57
Third Missionary Journey

AD 67
Paul's second imprisonment in Rome

AD 50-52
Second Missionary Journey

AD 57-59
Paul in prison in Caesarea

AD 62-64
?Letter to the Hebrews

AD 59-60
Voyage to Rome

AD 60-62
Paul's first imprisonment in Rome

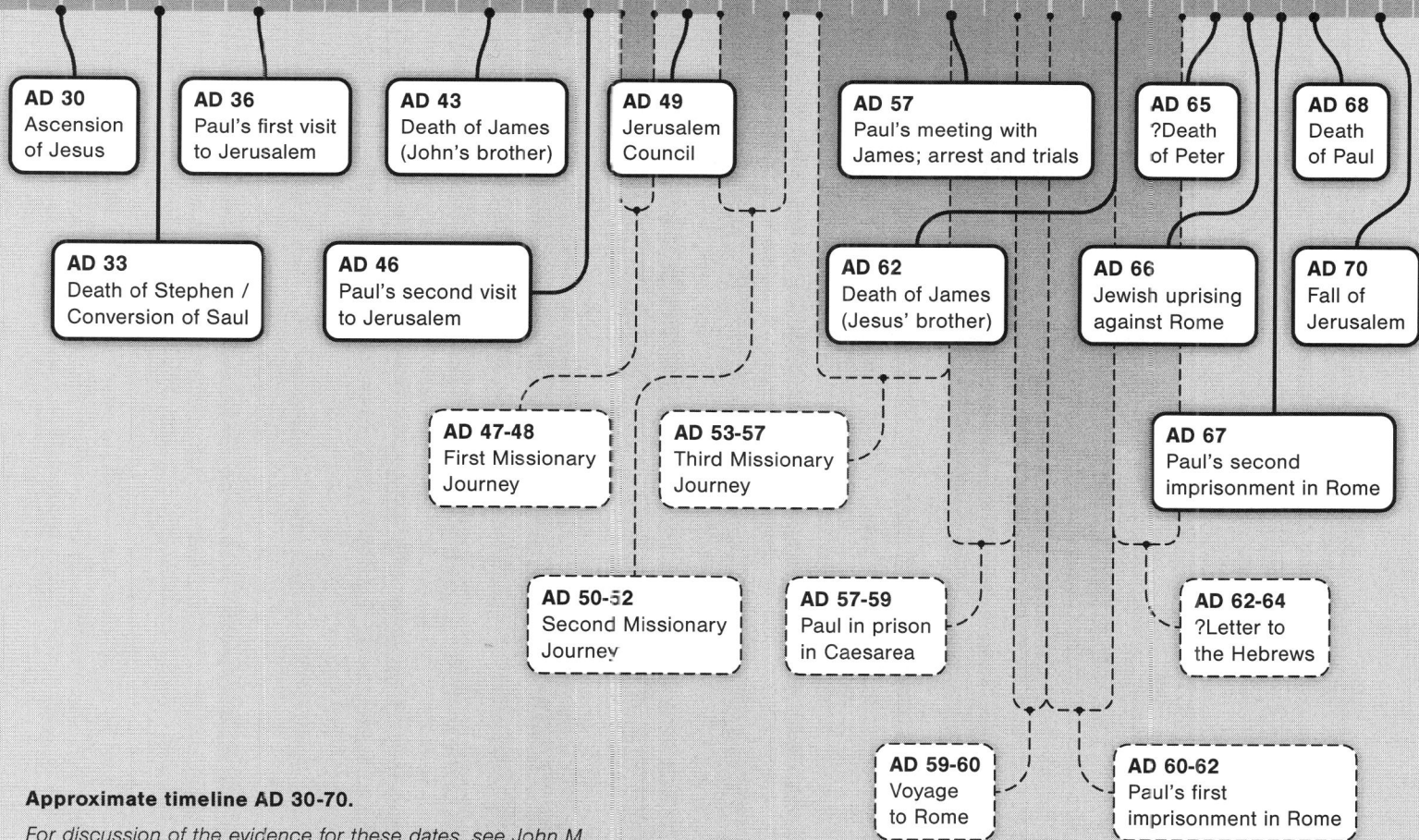

Approximate timeline AD 30-70.

*For discussion of the evidence for these dates, see John M. Hellawell, **Beginning at Jerusalem**, in particular Tables 4 & 13.*

Background in the Acts

THE JERUSALEM ECCLESIA

THE period covered by the Acts of the Apostles is from the ascension of Jesus (AD 30) to Paul's arrival in Rome after the journey recorded in Acts 27 and 28 (approximately AD 60). We have suggested that Hebrews was written between AD 62 and AD 64, which of course is later than the events in Acts – **but not so much later**. What we learn from Acts, and particularly what we can discover about the Jerusalem ecclesia, has to be relevant to our study of Hebrews.

Much has happened since the Eleven, after their Lord's ascension, first assembled in the upper room. As a result of the early preaching, the ecclesia in Jerusalem expanded and went through great changes; their relationship with non-believers, with the temple, and the Jewish priesthood increasingly came under strain. It is worth following the developments that led, finally and inevitably, to the separation of those of 'The Way' from the traditions of Jewish worship in which they had been brought up. Here are some of the key events:

1. At Pentecost, Peter and John preached in Jerusalem. The number of disciples is recorded as "about a hundred and twenty" (1:15). But, as a result of preaching, the numbers quickly grew: "That day about three thousand souls were added ... the Lord added to the church daily those who were being saved ... the number of the men came to be about five thousand ... believers were increasingly added to the Lord, multitudes of both men and women ... the number of the disciples was multiplying ... and a great many of the priests were obedient to the faith" (2:41,47; 4:4; 5:14; 6:1,7).

2. When the apostles were imprisoned, "an angel of the Lord opened the prison doors and brought them out, and said, Go, stand in the temple and speak to the people all the words of this life ... And daily, in the temple, and in every house, they did not cease teaching and preaching Jesus as the Christ" (5:19,20,42).

3. The believers came under attack from the temple authorities. Stephen was accused of speaking "blasphemous words against this holy place and the law; for we have heard him say that this Jesus of Nazareth will destroy this place and change the customs which Moses delivered to us" (6:9-14). Then follows Stephen's speech which showed, very pointedly, how that down the

THE TEMPLE AND SYNAGOGUES

The temple in Jerusalem was the focus of Jewish worship, but as a consequence of exile and dispersion, when Jews were cut off from their sanctuary, synagogues came into being. There is evidence of synagogues from about the 3rd century BC; they were places where Jews could gather for prayer and the reading of the Torah (but not for the feasts). The New Testament refers to Jesus teaching in the temple, but also in synagogues up and down the land. After the Lord's ascension, believers continued to worship and preach in the temple and in the synagogues: Paul confessed later that (as Saul) he "in every synagogue imprisoned and beat those who believed ... I punished them often in every synagogue" (Acts 22:19; 26:11). Eventually, however, as persecution increased, Christians had to find other places to meet: several times we read of "the ecclesia that is in their / your house" (e.g., 1 Corinthians 16:19; Philemon :2).

Ruin of a Jewish synagogue

ages faithful men of God – Abraham, Joseph, Moses, David and others – had acceptably worshipped God in places other than the temple at Jerusalem; and he concludes with a statement which cut the Jewish rulers to the heart: "The Most High does not dwell in temples made with hands" (7:48). Stephen was one of the first to acknowledge that the new community of Christ's followers no longer belonged in the temple.

4. As a consequence of Stephen's outspoken attack, "a great persecution arose against the church which was at Jerusalem; and they were all scattered throughout the regions of Judea and Samaria, except the apostles" (8:1). Saul, moreover, "made havoc of the church" (8:3). The ecclesia recovered, however, and when Saul was converted, "he was with them at Jerusalem, coming in and going out"; "Then the churches throughout all Judea, Galilee, and Samaria had peace and were edified ... were multiplied" (9:26-28,31).

5. Peter continues to take the lead in Acts 10-12, but before he preached to the Gentile Cornelius it needed the vision in Joppa to convince Peter that he "should not call any man common or unclean" (10:28). Peter was called to give account of his actions to the apostles and brethren in Judea who, receiving the joyous news of these latest conversions, "glorified God, saying, Then God has also granted to the Gentiles

repentance to life" (11:1,18). In spite of this breakthrough, "those who were scattered after the persecution that arose over Stephen ... preached the word to no one but the Jews only ... and a great number believed and turned to the Lord" (11:19-21).

6. As Paul comes on the scene and the missionary journeys begin, the spotlight shifts away from Jerusalem, though matters of doctrine continue to be referred to the elders at Jerusalem. Barnabas recruits Saul (who becomes Paul) and the First Missionary Journey takes the Gospel from Antioch in Syria to Cyprus and Asia Minor (chapters 13,14). Arriving back at Antioch, the apostles "reported all that God had done with them, and that He had opened the door of faith to the Gentiles" (14:27). After the Jerusalem Council (see "Judaisers and the Jerusalem Council" on page 12), the apostles set off on the Second Missionary Journey, taking the Gospel into Europe (15:36–18:22).

7. At the end of the Third Missionary Journey (18:23–21:15), Paul came to Jerusalem, carrying with him the 'great collection' which he had gathered from "Macedonia and Achaia ... for the poor among the saints who are in Jerusalem" (Romans 15:25-27; 1 Corinthians 16:1-3; 2 Corinthians 8,9). Poverty in the ecclesia at this time (and later) will have been at least partly the result of former priests and Levites withdrawing from service in the temple. Financial help

will have been very welcome, but Paul had reason to be nervous of the reception he might have, even as he handed over the collection: there were still some in Jerusalem who were suspicious of his activities. He

"Brethren, my heart's desire and prayer to God for Israel is that they may be saved. For I bear them witness that they have a zeal for God, but not according to knowledge." (Romans 10:1,2)

mentions that anxiety when writing to the Romans: "Strive together with me in prayers to God ... that I may be delivered from those in Judea who do not believe, and that my service for Jerusalem may be acceptable to the saints" (Romans 15:30,31). In the event, and no doubt helped by the warmth and enthusiasm of the delegates travelling with Paul, the "alms and offerings" were well received: "When we had come to Jerusalem, the brethren received us gladly" (Acts 21:17; 24:17).

8. A very significant incident is recorded in Acts 21. When the apostles returned to Jerusalem after the Third Missionary Journey, "Paul went in with us to James, and all the elders were present ... [Paul] told in detail those things which God had done among the Gentiles through his ministry. When they heard it, they glorified the Lord", but then went on to raise an urgent matter: "You see, brother, how many myriads of Jews there are who have believed, and they are all zealous for the law; but they have been informed about you that you teach all the Jews who are among the Gentiles to forsake Moses ... Therefore do what we tell you: We have four men who have taken a vow. Take them and be purified with them ... that all may know that those things of which they were informed concerning you are nothing, but that you yourself also walk orderly and keep the law" (21:17-24). Paul did what the elders requested – and the riot

that followed led to his arrest, trial, appeal to Caesar, and the journey to Rome.

9. There is little more that we can glean from Acts. Luke ends his account at the first arrest of Paul in Rome. In the few years that remained before the horrors of AD 70, the Jerusalem ecclesia will have faced the taunts and antagonism of Jews towards the Christian sect who were no longer regular worshippers in the temple, and who did not support their patriotic stand against the Romans.

10. After AD 70, the temple and the city lay in ruins, and the population was dispersed. The Jerusalem ecclesia was no more, but many members (following the advice of the Lord himself) fled "to the mountains" (Luke 21:21) – to Pella, east of Jordan. Sadly, there is reason to believe that, ignoring the appeals of the Letter to the Hebrews, some continued to observe the Law – while also meeting on the first day of the week to remember the Lord's death.

The Letter to the Hebrews would fit in the period following number 8 above. The readers were suffering persecution, they were being denied temple support, they were poor. But it was necessary that Christians should cease completely their observance of the Law. Worship in the temple precincts had always been a compromise; now they must "go forth ... bearing his reproach" (13:13).

JUDAISERS AND THE JERUSALEM COUNCIL

Paul (Saul) had been a Judaiser, fanatically opposed to the 'Way' being preached by the apostles of Jesus. But even after Paul's conversion, others continued to hinder the work, for example in Antioch in Pisidia: "When the Jews saw the multitudes, they were filled with envy; and contradicting and blaspheming, they opposed the things spoken by Paul" (Acts 13:45).

Tragically, however, even among some converts to the faith, Judaistic attitudes persisted. In Antioch in Syria, "certain men came down from Judea and taught the brethren, 'Unless you are circumcised according to the custom of Moses, you cannot be saved'" (Acts 15:1; cf. Galatians 2:12). These "certain men" could accept the idea of Gentile converts, but only if such converts were circumcised and kept to the Law. (This emphasis on circumcision led to the use of the term "the circumcision" to describe hardline Jews.) The Letter to the Galatians tells us of the crisis of faith that arose in Galatia as a result of the subversive work of these Judaisers (including "false brethren secretly brought in", 2:4), and Paul chides the believers: "How is it that you turn again to the weak and beggarly elements, to which you desire again to be in bondage ... I am afraid for you, lest I have laboured for you in vain" (4:9-11).

The Antioch ecclesia, unable to settle the matter, "determined that Paul and Barnabas and certain others of them should go up to Jerusalem, to the apostles and elders, about this question" (Acts 15:2). What followed is referred to as the Jerusalem Council (or Conference), at which there was "much dispute". Agreement was reached, however, and James summed up the conclusions as follows: "I judge that we should not trouble those from among the Gentiles who are turning to God [i.e. trouble them to keep the Law] but that we write to them ..." (15:19,20). What then follows is guidance to Gentile believers to abstain from practices offensive to Jews; but otherwise they were not required to be circumcised or to keep the Law of Moses.

This message no doubt clarified the situation for Gentile converts. For Jewish believers, however, the problem did not altogether go away. In his Letter to the Romans, Paul chides those Jews who "boast in the law" (2:23); and he has to deal with "disputes over doubtful things" – food laws, and the observing of special days (14:1-6). To the Colossians he writes, "Let no one judge you in food or drink, or regarding a festival (feast day) or a new moon or sabbaths" (2:16).

In Jerusalem, no doubt more than anywhere else, converted Jews still resisted making that final break with the Law. For them, being already circumcised, circumcision was not an issue (it does not arise in Hebrews), but breaking those ties with the temple was difficult. James appears to have been reluctant to say how and when that separation should occur; he even persuades Paul to join men taking a vow in the temple (see No. 8 above). But very soon after this (as we suggest in the next chapter) the break came, partly forced upon the believers by the worsening political situation, and also surely influenced by the Letter to the Hebrews.

The problem

LETTING GO OF THE LAW

WHAT JESUS HAD SAID ABOUT THE LAW

Jesus was above the Law: he touched and healed the leper, and the woman with a flow of blood; he touched and raised the dead. In his parables he taught that the Law was like an old garment or an old wineskin – no longer fit for purpose. The parable of the Good Samaritan pointed the finger at the priest and the Levite who, seeing the man who had been left half dead, had nothing to offer him but "passed by on the other side" (Luke 10:31,32). The parable of the Lost Son portrayed the **older** brother, typical of those who kept rigidly to the Law, as the one who was truly lost. In the parable of the Rich Man and Lazarus, Jesus inserts the telling phrase: "They have Moses and the prophets; let them hear them" (Luke 16:29).

HEBREWS was written to believers who evidently had learned and accepted the Gospel, had been baptized, had begun their walk as disciples of Christ, had been zealous for good works, and had even suffered for their faith. They were, however, still participating in temple worship and the observance of the Law and needed some persuading to let it go. If only they could do this, their growth in the Gospel would be much more rapid.

The Hebrews' problem was how to turn their backs on all they had loved as Jews, and become outcasts from the temple and from Jewish society. Jesus, by giving himself as the perfect sacrifice for sin, had done away with the need for the Law, the priesthood and the temple. He, the risen Christ, had entered through the veil into the Holiest and was now High Priest at God's right hand, their mediator and intercessor. The law of Moses, which had been the foundation of Israel's life for so long (and had itself pointed forward to the work of Christ), had nothing more to offer. They had to let it go!

The final break with the temple

But we have to ask the question: Had any clear advice been given to the Jewish believers in Jerusalem? Had the ecclesia come to any decision whether and when they should forsake the temple and no longer observe the Law of Moses? The Jerusalem Council (AD 49) had agreed on guidelines for the Gentiles (Acts 15:6-29; 21:25), but did not discuss what Jews should do.

In the absence of some directive from the apostles, it was understandable that members of the Jerusalem ecclesia(s) would continue their attendance in the temple. Even Paul, at the end of the Second Missionary Journey, not only undertook a vow in Cenchrea, but then left Ephesus, saying, "I must by all means **keep this coming feast** in Jerusalem" (Acts 18:18,21). And later, after the Third Missionary Journey, Paul (at the elders' request) agreed to accompany into the temple four men who had undertaken a vow (Acts 21:20-24). As late as AD 57, therefore, Jewish Christians (at least in Jerusalem) continued to adhere to the Law.

How and when did things change? Sooner or later, Christian converts must have begun to feel uncomfortable worshipping with unbelieving Jews. The conversion to the Christian faith of "a great many of the priests" (Acts 6:7), and the refusal of believers to support the patriotic uprising which was beginning to gain momentum, will inevitably have led the apostles and elders to plan for withdrawal from the temple.

We have very little information, but we can speculate that James the Lord's brother, as leader and spokesman for the Jerusalem ecclesia, had been advising brothers and sisters to prepare for that day. James, as we know from his epistle (e.g., 2:14-26), accepted that the Law of Moses had been replaced by faith in Christ, and he will have felt a responsibility on his shoulders to 'wean' the ecclesia from the old Law. When Paul was in Jerusalem, we can imagine James discussing strategy with him (the two men had known each other from the earliest days after Paul's conversion – see Galatians 1:19; 2:9).

> "Has not God chosen the poor of this world to be rich in faith and heirs of the kingdom which He promised to those who love Him?" (James 2:5)

Following the arrest of Paul, and the uproar in Jerusalem (Acts 21-23), hostility grew and brothers and sisters would have been increasingly unwelcome in Jewish religious circles. The time had come to "go forth".

Painful separation

So did they just walk away? Some, we can be sure, were only too ready to make the break,

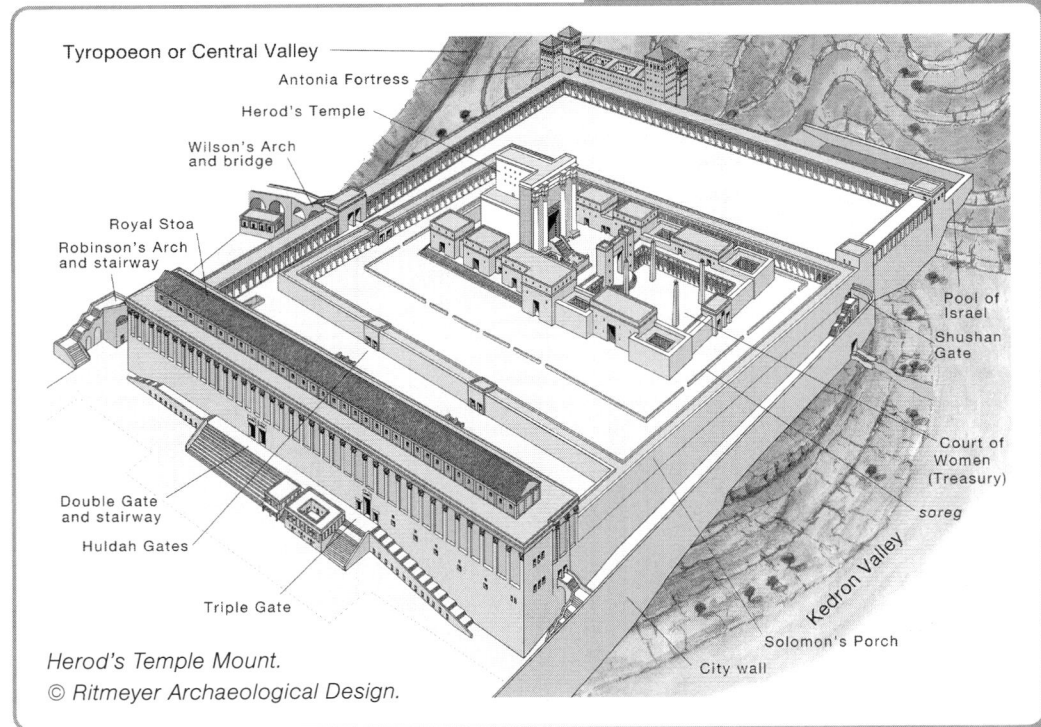

Tyropoeon or Central Valley
Antonia Fortress
Herod's Temple
Wilson's Arch and bridge
Royal Stoa
Robinson's Arch and stairway
Double Gate and stairway
Huldah Gates
Triple Gate
Pool of Israel
Shushan Gate
Court of Women (Treasury)
soreg
Kedron Valley
Solomon's Porch
City wall

Herod's Temple Mount.
© Ritmeyer Archaeological Design.

accepting that in Christ they no longer had need of priests and sacrifices; these would have turned away from the temple without a backward glance. But others were not ready. Remember the words of the Jerusalem elders in Acts 21:20 – "You see, brother, how many myriads of Jews there are who have believed, **and they are all zealous for the law**". Paul's action in agreeing to go into the temple was designed to reassure

"The Letter to the Hebrews is the divine call to leave Judaism completely. Apart from such a command the Jewish believer would not have separated himself from the rest of his fellow Jews. Hitherto he had continued to meet in the temple and to follow the temple services ... The time had come for a formal and definite repeal of the law" (John Carter, *The Letter to the Hebrews*, 1947 edition, pages 7 & 178).

those "myriads of Jews", though it may actually have encouraged some of them to think that they could continue to observe the Law. Indeed, why could they not observe their Christian faith alongside the feasts and sacrifices?

What was to be done? A crisis was looming and urgent action was necessary to encourage Jewish believers – the Hebrews – to make that final break with the temple. Paul, incidentally, would have seen the situation from the perspective of ecclesias in the Gentile world, who would have been surprised – perhaps shocked – that believers in Jerusalem were still adhering to the Law.

James (to continue our speculation) may have sought Paul's help – even suggesting that he should write a letter to those in Jerusalem who were still resisting change. However, events then overtook Paul. He was arrested and might not have had opportunity to write the letter until he was in prison in Caesarea (AD 57-59), or in Rome (AD 60-62), or possibly not until he was released from his first Roman imprisonment. With the passage of time, of course, the situation in Jerusalem is bound to have changed: some members of the ecclesia may still not have broken their ties with the Law; others, having once left it all behind, may actually have drifted back to the temple. Reports reaching Paul around this time may have been the trigger for him to write our Letter.

We have ventured into the realms of speculation, and there must still be considerable

uncertainty about what finally provoked Paul to write.

Harsh words or sympathy?

The Gospel meant a painful separation, and before we criticise the Hebrews too harshly we should spare a thought for their predicament. They could be forgiven, up to a point, for having a lingering affection for the temple – it was, after all, a sanctuary built for the glory of God; it was where the Lord himself often taught and where the apostles preached. When most of them were first baptized, the practices of the Law continued to be part of their normal religious life. Now they were to be "strangers and pilgrims", ostracised by colleagues, friends and family members, and enduring loss of income and esteem.

"They will put you out of the synagogues; yes, the time is coming that whoever kills you will think that he offers God service." (John 16:2)

Of course, if they were indeed drawing back from Christ and 'forsaking the assembling of themselves together", they deserved to be rebuked. But if they were merely bewildered at the turn of events, then what they required was a clear but compassionate reminder of the new and better things that were theirs in Christ. That, of course, is exactly what the writer to the Hebrews provides: warnings for any who were reluctant to leave the Law behind, but gentle and persuasive exhortation for those who had made the break but were struggling to cope.

How will the writer tackle the problem?

Departures from the faith can be tackled in different ways. Sometimes, it is appropriate to come straight to the point with robust criticism. One example of this is Paul's approach to the Galatians: "I marvel that you are turning away so soon ... if we, or an angel from heaven, preach any other gospel to you than what we have preached to you, let him be accursed" (1:6-8). Even more vigorously: "O foolish Galatians! Who has bewitched you ...?" (3:1). The Hebrews were in a different situation, which called for compassion and tact rather than condemnation.

For the two on the road to Emmaus, Jesus' approach was one of gentle chiding: "O foolish ones, and slow of heart to believe in all that the prophets have spoken! Ought not the Christ to have suffered these things and to enter into his glory?"

(Luke 24:25,26)

It is interesting that the writer is sparing in his use of "you" when referring to his readers; he is much more inclined to speak of "we" and "us". He uses "you" when complimenting them (e.g., 6:9-12; 10:32-26) and in some of his exhortations (e.g., 3:12,13; 12:3-25; 13:1-25)

but, especially when he is being critical of the Hebrews, he often uses "we". Thus:

- "Therefore **we** must give the more earnest heed to the things **we** have heard, lest **we** drift away" (2:1).

- "Let **us** therefore be diligent to enter that rest, lest anyone fall according to the same example of disobedience" (4:11).

- "Let **us** hold fast the confession of **our** hope without wavering, for he who promised is faithful. And let **us** consider **one another** in order to stir up love and good works, not forsaking the assembling of **ourselves** together. For if **we** sin wilfully after **we** have received the knowledge of the truth, there no longer remains a sacrifice for sins" (10:23-26).

- "Therefore, since **we** are receiving a kingdom which cannot be shaken, let **us** have grace, by which **we** may serve God acceptably with reverence and godly fear. For **our** God is a consuming fire" (12:28-29).

By his use of "we", "us", "our" etc. the writer is associating himself with his readers and softening his tone. He is certainly not wishing to 'throw his weight around'. This surely is part of the reason for omitting his name at the start of the Letter. But Paul is self-effacing not just in writing anonymously to the Hebrews. We are used to Paul, at the outset of nearly all of his letters, making reference to his apostleship. In this letter, by contrast, he drops both his name

> "For Christ is the end of the law for righteousness to everyone who believes."   (Romans 10:4)

and any reference to his apostolic authority: he is associating himself humbly with his fellow-countrymen, writing, as it were, as one of them.

The other technique, calculated to avoid alienating his readers, is for the writer to tackle their mistaken attitudes indirectly rather than head-on. For example:

- Instead of bluntly dismissing the Law, he shows that Jesus was superior to the angels by whom the Law was originally given.

- Instead of arguing directly against the priesthood of Aaron, he demonstrates the superiority of the earlier – and continuing – order of Melchizedek.

- Rather than appear to be denigrating temple worship, he focuses instead on the tabernacle.

- Rather than attack the works of the Law, he concentrates on showing that faith is better.

As we open the book, we see how masterfully the writer sets about persuading the Hebrews to break finally with the old and embrace the new.

Hebrews chapter 1

"GOD HAS SPOKEN BY HIS SON"

WITHOUT any greeting or preamble, the writer to the Hebrews launches straight into his theme. The letter commences with a majestic opening statement about the nature of God's purpose through His Son:

> *"God, who at various times and in various ways spoke in time past to the fathers by the prophets, has in these last days spoken to us by His Son, whom He has appointed heir of all things, through whom also He made the worlds; who being the brightness of His glory and the express image of His person, and upholding all things by the word of his power, when he had by himself purged our sins, sat down at the right hand of the Majesty on high, having become so much better than the angels, as he has by inheritance obtained a more excellent name than they."* (1:1-4)

Perhaps we should not even try to condense this glorious summary of the Gospel any further, but the essence can actually be stated in the six words of our chapter heading: *"God has spoken by His Son"*. This short phrase expresses the fact that God's plan of redemption reached its finality in Christ.

God spoke at creation. He spoke in the eternal promises to the patriarchs. He spoke in the types and shadows of the Law. The Psalmist spoke of the Son at God's right hand. God spoke through the prophets concerning the coming of the Servant, the Lamb, the King. Throughout the pages of the Old Testament, God was speaking and a picture of the Christ was being built up – a jigsaw of many pieces that would reveal the complete picture only when Jesus came. The phrases below show how Hebrews repeatedly emphasises the idea of God's **voice speaking** His **word**.

The Hebrews were lingering in the past; they had not truly moved forward to embrace God's

> "Again he sent other servants ... Then last of all he sent his son to them ..." (Matthew 21:36,37)

- "God has **spoken**" (1:1,2).
- "The **word** of his power" (1:3).
- "The **word spoken** through angels" (2:2).
- "**Spoken** by the Lord" (2:3).
- "If you will hear His **voice**" (3:7,15; 4:7).
- "The **word** which they heard did not profit them" (4:2).
- "The **word** of God is living and powerful ..." (4:12).
- "Tasted the good **word** of God" (6:5).
- "The **word** of the oath" (7:28).
- "The worlds were framed by the **word** of God" (11:3).
- "The **voice of words** ... begged that the **word** should not be **spoken** to them anymore" (12:19).
- "Do not refuse Him who **speaks**" (12:25).
- "whose **voice** then shook the earth" (12:26).
- "Remember those ... who have **spoken** the **word** of God to you" (13:7).

- "God in tyme past **diversly and many wayes** spake unto the fathers by prophets: but in these last dayes he hath spoken unto us by hys Sonne ..." (Tyndale).

- "God, who **at sundry times and in divers manners** spake in time past ..." (KJV).

- "**In many parts, and many ways**, God of old having spoken to the fathers in the prophets ..." (Young's Literal).

- "**Many were the forms and fashions** in which God spoke of old ..." (Moffatt).

- "God, after He spoke long ago to the fathers in the prophets **in many portions and in many ways** ..." (NASB).

- "Long ago, **at many times and in many ways**, God spoke ..." (ESV).

full and final revelation. The epistle is about Jesus Christ, the Son of God, and the opening verses wonderfully summarise what he achieved. Chapter 1 starts with a portrait of the Son, and moves on to consider his exaltedness above the angels.

"At various times and in various ways"

In its original form the epistle commenced with the above phrase – in Greek, *polumerōs kai polutropōs*. A few English versions, e.g., Young's Literal Translation and Moffatt, are faithful to this word order (see side panel). The phrase "at various times and in various ways" is actually key to the message of Hebrews, because it stresses that God's revelation was not a 'one-time', 'one-place' occurrence (at Sinai) but a process throughout the aeons of time – through patriarchs, priests, psalmists and prophets, and finally through the perfect manifestation of the Father in the Son, the Word made flesh.

Stephen, in his speech reviewing Israel's history, had made a similar point (Acts 7): in every age and in a variety of places (Mesopotamia, Haran, Egypt. Midian, Sinai, Babylon), God had been worshipped. The temple in Jerusalem was not the only place of acceptable worship. Paul, although he rebelled against Stephen's words at the time, will have kept them in his heart, and it is not surprising that Hebrews contains echoes of that speech.

Though the Hebrews believed in Jesus, they could not see that "the word spoken by the Lord" (2:3) had now fulfilled and superseded the word through Moses. Paul needs to deal with their short-sightedness. He focuses first on the exalted status of the Son of God. (Interestingly, it is not until chapter 2 that he actually names the name of Jesus.)

Seven phrases

That majestic opening statement is followed by seven short phrases defining the nature and work of the Son:

1. "Whom He has appointed heir of all things"

2. "Through whom also He made the worlds"

3. "Who being the brightness of His glory"

4. "And the express image of His person"

5. "Upholding all things by the word of his power"

Πολυμερῶς καὶ πολυτρόπως

The first three words in the Greek version of Hebrews: polumerōs kai polutropōs

6. "When he had by himself purged our sins"

7. "Sat down at the right hand of the Majesty on high"

The Hebrews did not seem to appreciate the Son's exalted position in the divine plan. They needed to be reminded that Jesus had always been in the mind of the Father, destined for the highest status in God's purpose.

"Heir of all things" tells us straight away that all the purposes of God pointed to the Son, and the kingdom that God planned would be his inheritance:

"I will give you the nations for your inheritance, and the ends of the earth for your possession." (Psalm 2:8)

"Through whom also He made the worlds" reinforces the point that, from the very beginning, Jesus was in the mind of the Creator – proved by the quotation from Psalm 102: "You, Lord, in the beginning laid the foundation of the earth, and the heavens are the work of Your hands ..." (1:10-12). There is no suggestion here of the pre-existence of Christ, but rather that God had the Son in view when the heavens and the earth were made, when man was formed from the dust, and when the aeons of history were foreseen.

The Son is *the brightness of [God's] glory"*: Instead of "brightness", some versions have "radiance" or "effulgence", describing the intensity and beauty of the glory of God manifested by His Son: "We beheld his glory,

the glory as of the only begotten of the Father, full of grace and truth" (John 1:14).

"The express image of His person": The two words "express image" are translated from a single Greek word *charakter*, which originally referred to the impression made by a die or stamp: "[He is] the **exact imprint** of his nature" (ESV). The word at the end of the phrase has to do with 'substance', 'foundation' or 'reality': neither "person" nor "nature" quite catches the meaning. Jesus Christ represented the **reality** of God to man.

> "He is the image of the invisible God, the firstborn of all creation."
> (Colossians 1:15, ESV)

"Upholding all things by the word of his power": Is Jesus here being contrasted with Moses, who confessed to God: "I am not able to **bear** all these people alone" (Numbers 11:14)? Jesus bears and upholds all things. "He is before all things, and in him all things consist [ESV, hold together]" (Colossians 1:17). The Father has given the risen Christ all power: "All authority has been given to me in heaven and on earth" (Matthew 28:18).

"He by himself purged our sins": This phrase reminds the Hebrews that the sacrifices and feasts of the Law had been made obsolete. Even the Day of Atonement when the High Priest, once a year, made purification for all Israel – "that you

> "It is the God who commanded light to shine out of darkness, who has shone in our hearts to give the light of the knowledge of the glory of God in the face of Jesus Christ."
> (2 Corinthians 4:6)

may be clean from all your sins before the LORD" (Leviticus 16 30) – was now redundant. By his sacrifice, "once for all", Jesus has provided the way for lasting forgiveness. This topic will of course be developed later on in the epistle.

"Sat down at the right hand of the majesty on high": Because of his place in the Father's purpose; because of the perfection of his character; and because he had conquered sin and given himself as an atonement for sin, the Son is worthy to sit at God's right hand.

So ends the first sentence of this amazing Letter, a sentence which can be abbreviated to the following:

"God has spoken by His Son who sat down at the right hand of the Majesty on high."

This 'simple' statement says so much. In particular, the phrase "sat down at the right hand of the Majesty on high" takes us to Psalm 110, a psalm which is at the heart of this Epistle:

'The LORD said to my Lord, **'Sit at my right hand'** ... Rule in the midst of your enemies! ... 'You are a priest forever according to the order of Melchizedek' ... **The Lord is at your right hand** ... He shall judge among the nations." (Psalm 110)

Here is the essence of the Letter to the Hebrews: God has spoken through His Son, His heir, the perfect revelation of the Father, the Saviour who has purged our sins, the Lord exalted to sit at God's right hand, the Priest after the order of Melchizedek, the King who comes

to rule and judge the nations. These are the truths foreshadowed in Psalm 110 which will be expanded and expounded as the Letter proceeds.

However familiar we are with Hebrews, it is good to reflect on what **we** understand about the work of Jesus. How would **we** describe him? We would probably emphasise his origins as the Seed of the woman, the Prophet like Moses, the Lamb of God, the suffering Servant; we would explain how he was born in Bethlehem, went about teaching and healing, was crucified, raised from the dead, and ascended to the Father. Some of these aspects are covered in the opening verses of Hebrews, but the reader is taken to a higher plane; the Lord Jesus Christ is portrayed in an eternal context – which is precisely where the Hebrews fell short in their understanding. They had believed in Jesus but had not really acknowledged his position as the exalted Son of God.

Sadly, for many in this world, Jesus remains the 'babe in a manger'; people are not prepared to acknowledge him as Redeemer and King. But we too can be in danger of understanding the facts about Jesus, and yet not fully appreciate the exaltedness of the One who is "worthy to receive ... honour and glory and blessing" (Revelation 5:12).

Better than the angels

Now the argument takes a very subtle turn. One more phrase is added to the seven we have

"Therefore God also has highly exalted him and given him the name which is above every name, that at the name of Jesus every knee should bow."

(Philippians 2:9,10)

already noted. This eighth phrase contrasts the risen Christ with angels: *"Having become so much better than the angels."* This final phrase spells out the truth that because of all that God had predestined for His Son, Christ has *"a more excellent name than they"*.

But why suddenly introduce angels? The answer to that question is that if Christ was "better than the angels", then the Gospel he preached must be superior to "the word spoken through angels", that is, the Law given by angels to Moses. Paul wrote to the Galatians: "What purpose then does the law serve? It was added because of transgressions, till the Seed should come to whom the promise was made; and it was **appointed through angels** by the hand of a mediator" (Galatians 3:19; cf. Acts 7:53). The Seed had now come, so adherence to the Law was no longer required.

The verses which follow (1:5-13) quote seven significant Old Testament passages:

1. Psalm 2:7 – *"You are My Son, today I have begotten you"*.

2. 2 Samuel 7:14 – *"I will be to him a Father, and he shall be to Me a Son"*.

3. Deuteronomy 32:43 (LXX) – *"But when He again brings the firstborn [cf. Psalm 89:27] into the world, He says: Let all the angels of God worship him"*.

4. Psalm 104:4 – *"Who makes His angels spirits and His ministers a flame of fire"*.

5. Psalm 45:6,7 – *"Your throne, O God, is forever and ever ... You have loved righteousness ... Therefore God, your God, has anointed you with the oil of gladness more than your companions"*.

6. Psalm 102:25-27 – *"You, LORD, in the beginning laid the foundation of the earth ... They will perish ... they will be changed. But you are the same, and your years will not fail"*.

Finally, Paul adds Psalm 110, alluded to in verse 3 but now quoted. (Psalm 110 is

> "Rejoice, ye heavens, with him, and let all the angels of God worship him; rejoice ye Gentiles, with his people, and let all the sons of God strengthen themselves in him."
> (Deuteronomy 32:43, Septuagint)

FALSE IDEAS ABOUT ANGELS

Before we go on, it is worth asking: Did the Hebrews see Jesus as an angel? Does the focus on angels at the end of chapter 1 and on into chapter 2 suggest that some in the ecclesia were influenced by the false thinking about angels that abounded in the world of the 1st century? The Greeks, for example, had the idea that between God and man there were successive 'orders' of angels acting as mediators, an idea developed by the Gnostics and hinted at in Colossians 2:18. And many Jews, following the notions of the Jewish philosopher Philo, believed that angels had not only been involved in creation, but had been appointed to have authority over the 'world to come'. At the end of the epistle, the writer warns his readers against being "carried about with various and strange doctrines" (13:9), and perhaps these included heretical ideas about angels. New Testament teaching regarding angels is clear:

- As "ministering spirits", angels were not to be worshipped (Revelation 19:10; 22:8,9);

- The Galatians (1:8) were warned not to be led astray, though "we, or an angel from heaven, preach any other gospel";

- Paul taught that "we shall judge angels" (1 Corinthians 6:3);

- The things which the prophets of Israel searched, were "things which angels desire to look into" (1 Peter 1:10-12) – angels are not omniscient.

REFERENCES TO PSALM 110

As we have seen, Psalm 110:1 is first quoted in Hebrews to show how the Son was exalted to sit at God's right hand; that theme returns in later chapters, while in chapters 5 – 7 the focus shifts to verse 4 of Psalm 110, in connection with the priesthood of Christ:

- "Sit at my right hand, till I make your enemies your footstool" (1:13).
- "You are a priest forever according to the order of Melchizedek" (5:6,10; 6:20; 7:17,21).
- "A High Priest, who is seated at the right hand of the throne of the Majesty in the heavens" (8:1).
- "This man, after he had offered one sacrifice for sins forever, sat down at the right hand of God" (10:12).
- "Jesus ... who for the joy that was set before him endured the cross ... and has sat down at the right hand of the throne of God" (12:2).

    Psalm 110 is the watershed for the concept of Messiah as king and priest.

the most quoted psalm in Hebrews – in fact the most frequently quoted in the New Testament.)

7. Psalm 110:1 – *"Sit at My right hand, till I make your enemies your footstool"*.

Like all Jews, the Hebrews will have known and loved their Old Testament scriptures, especially the psalms, and surely could not fail to acknowledge the power of Paul's argument. He was citing scriptures which showed that Jesus was superior to the angels and from these he proves that:

- No angel had ever been addressed as "my Son" or had God as his Father (Hebrews 1:5).

- The angels are called upon to worship the Son (1:6).
- Angels are spirit beings and servants of God (1:7).
- The Son can properly be referred to as "God"; his throne and sceptre prove his authority; he is exalted because of his righteousness (1:8,9).
- The Son was in the mind of the Father from the foundation of the heavens and earth, and though they might pass away, "you are the same, and your years will not fail" (1:10-12; see comment on 13:8).
- No angel is qualified to sit on God's right hand (1:13).

There is, incidentally, no reason to be worried about the references to the Son as "God". Did not Jesus himself say, "If He called them gods, to whom the word of God came (and the Scripture cannot be broken), do you say of him whom the Father sanctified and sent into the world, 'You are blaspheming,' because I said, 'I am the Son of God'?" (John 10:35,36).

The quotation from Psalm 102, besides adding to the proofs of the greater standing of the Son, has an extra thrust. Would the Hebrews have noticed the implication of phrases like *"They will perish ... they will all grow old like a garment ... they will be changed"*? This was a not-so-subtle reference to the perishing of the Law, and its replacement by the Gospel. The Lord in his parables had spoken of the uselessness of sewing a piece of unshrunk cloth on an old garment; of putting new wine into old wineskins (Mark 2:21,22). The old order – the Law – was obsolete: "Now what is becoming obsolete and growing old is ready to vanish away" (8:13).

The chapter concludes with a concise summary of the work of angels: *"Are they not all ministering spirits sent forth to minister for those who will inherit salvation?"* (1:14). The angels are servants, and though they are indeed referred to in the Old Testament as "sons of God", no angel could be called "**the** Son of God".

Chapter 2 will make it very clear that, whilst Jesus was "made a little lower than the angels, for the suffering of death", he is now exalted above the angels.

POINTS TO PONDER:

1. Suggest possible reasons why the author did not introduce himself or greet his readers.

2. Take a blank sheet of paper / computer document and try, in your own words, to summarise the nature and work of Jesus Christ. The exercise will remind you of the many names and roles of our Lord.

3. What are angels doing now?

4. List the occurrences of "better" in Hebrews, starting with "better than the angels" (1:4).

Hebrews chapter 2

"MADE LIKE HIS BRETHREN"

CHAPTER 2 continues to prove the superiority of Christ to the angels, pointing out first of all that the Gospel (the word spoken through Christ) has so much more authority than the Law of Moses (the word spoken through angels):

> "Therefore we must give the more earnest heed to the things we have heard, lest we drift away. For if the word spoken through angels proved steadfast, and every transgression and disobedience received a just reward, how shall we escape if we neglect so great a salvation, which at the first began to be spoken by the Lord, and was confirmed to us by those who heard him, God also bearing witness both with signs and wonders, with various miracles, and gifts of the Holy Spirit, according to His own will?" (2:1-4)

"Therefore ..."

Time and again in Hebrews, doctrinal discussion is immediately followed by exhortation – and that, of course, is as it should be. Bible exposition is not just theology; it must impact on the disciple's life. At critical points in the Letter, then, we have the word "therefore", leading into an exhortation based on what has just been expounded. Chapters 2, 3, 4, 6 and 12 all open with "Therefore", and we should look out for other occurrences in 4:11,16; 10:19,35; 12:12,28; 13:13,15 – in total, a dozen 'calls to action'!

"Give the more earnest heed ... lest we drift away" is the first of many exhortations to hold fast and not to draw back. It is also the first warning of the consequences of drifting: for if the law (the word through angels) judged "every transgression and disobedience" and could not be ignored, "how shall we escape if we neglect so great a salvation", spoken by no less than the Son of God himself? Many of them had heard the Gospel from apostles who received it from the Master; many had personally witnessed the "signs, wonders, miracles and gifts of the Holy Spirit" which testified to the greater authority of Christ. They had believed in Jesus, but instead of giving him their total allegiance they were still allowing the Law to rule their lives.

The writer now introduces another Old Testament passage as proof that God "has not put the world to come ... in subjection to angels" (2:5).

"One testified in a certain place, saying: 'What is man that You are mindful of him, or the son of man that You take care of him? You have made him a little lower than the angels; You

NAUTICAL LANGUAGE?

The author may have intended a nautical metaphor in verse 1. The following paraphrase has been suggested:

"Therefore, we must the more eagerly anchor our lives to the things that we have been taught lest the ship of life drift past the harbour and be wrecked." (William Barclay, *The Daily Study Bible*)

25

have crowned him with glory and honour ... You have put all things in subjection under his feet'." (2:6-8; Psalm 8:4-6)

The language takes us back, not just to Psalm 8, but to creation and to the instruction God gave to Adam and Eve to "be fruitful and multiply ... **have dominion** ... over every living thing that moves on the earth" (Genesis 1:28). This was the responsibility laid upon Adam and his descendants – but mankind failed to live up to it:

"We do not yet see all things put under him." (2:8)

There is, however, One who has proved worthy to fulfil the prophecy of Psalm 8: Jesus, **the** Son of Man, the "last Adam". He is the great exception; he has conquered and has been crowned:

"But we see Jesus, who was made a little lower than the angels, for the suffering of death crowned with glory and honour, that he, by the grace of God, might taste death for everyone." (2:9)

Daniel foresaw this in a vision: "Behold, One like the **Son of Man**, coming with the clouds of heaven! He came to the Ancient of Days, and they brought him near before Him. Then to him was given **dominion and glory** and a kingdom" (Daniel 7:13,14). The Lord Jesus Christ still awaits the time when his full authority will be exercised in the world (as the quotation from 1 Corinthians 15, alongside, also shows), but ultimately there will be *"nothing that is not put under him"* (verse 8).

"When I consider Your heavens ... What is man ...?" (Psalm 8:3,4)

"But we see Jesus" (2:9): We have waited until halfway through chapter 2 of Hebrews before the name "Jesus" is mentioned. When the epistle was first read out aloud, one can imagine an almost startled reaction at the mention of this name – startled, because the readers might not immediately connect Psalm 8 with the man from Nazareth. They might be reluctant to acknowledge that the Messiah also had to be Son of Man. But Jesus was mortal and must himself be saved from death (see 5:7) before he could save others. They are made perfect only because the captain of their salvation has "taste[d] death for everyone".

Had they really not grasped the fact that Messiah had to suffer? Jews could not cope

"Then comes the end, when he delivers the kingdom to God the Father, when he puts an end to all rule and all authority and power. For he must reign till he has put all enemies under his feet. The last enemy that will be destroyed is death" (1 Corinthians 15:24-26; see also Ephesians 1:20-22).

"A LITTLE LOWER THAN THE ANGELS"

In the original Hebrew of Psalm 8:5, the word is *Elohim*; in the Greek Septuagint, the word is "angels". There is no contradiction, for *Elohim* can, depending on the context, refer to 'angels'.

THE SUFFERING SERVANT

It would have been possible for the writer to the Hebrews, using Psalm 8, to concentrate on the glory of the risen Christ. After all, his main message in these early chapters is to show that Jesus is exalted, superior to the angels, better than Moses, a better High Priest etc. Why, then, would he wish to dwell on the humiliation of the Saviour? The answer is clear: Christ first had to be "despised and rejected by men" before he could "see the labour of his soul, and be satisfied" (Isaiah 53:3,11). Suffering had to come first; the glory would follow (1 Peter 1:11).

The point is powerfully made in chapter 2, but the sufferings of Christ continue to be emphasised throughout the epistle:

- "... to make the captain of their salvation perfect through sufferings" (2:10).
- "... in that he himself has suffered, being tempted" (2:18).
- "... in all points tempted as we are" (4:15).
- "... learned obedience by the things which he suffered" (5 8).
- "... would have had to suffer often ... but now ... once to bear the sins of many" (9:26-28).
- "... endured the cross, despising the shame, and has sat down at the right hand of the throne of God" (12:2)
- "... Jesus also, that he might sanctify the people with his own blood, suffered outside the gate" (13:12).

with the idea of a crucified Messiah: "Christ crucified [is] to the Jews a stumbling block and to the Greeks foolishness" (1 Corinthians 1:23). This difficulty goes back to the days when Jesus walked with his disciples. When the Master spoke of his impending death, Peter "began to rebuke him, saying, Far be it from you, Lord; this shall not happen to you!" (Matthew 16:22). And after his resurrection, the Lord chided the two who were walking to Emmaus: "Ought not the Christ to have suffered these things and to enter into his glory?" (Luke 24:26). When Paul wrote to the Hebrews, there were evidently still some who were slow to comprehend the need for Christ to suffer.

The cross before the crown

The Hebrews had to learn that before the Messiah could be "crowned with glory and honour" – and before he could bring other "sons to glory" – he had to be brought low. In the very section where the writer is driving home the truth that Jesus is superior to the angels, he nonetheless has to point out that "for the suffering of death" Jesus was "made a little [some versions read, 'for a little while'] lower than the angels". The cross must come before the crown. This same principle is there in Philippians: "He humbled himself and

Victor's crown (*stephanos*)

became obedient to the point of death, even the death of the cross. Therefore God also has highly exalted him" (Philippians 2:8,9).

> "Though he was crucified in weakness, yet he lives by the power of God."
> (2 Corinthians 13:4)

Wonderfully, it is all *"by the grace of God"*. By the grace of God, our Lord tasted death for everyone (2:9). Of course, Jesus offered himself freely, willingly, obediently; but the work of saving mankind was ultimately God's work: salvation is "by the grace of God". Verse 10 continues to explain this: *"For it was fitting for Him* [God], *for whom are all things and by whom are all things, in bringing many sons to glory, to make the captain of their salvation perfect through sufferings."* Truly, **"God** was in Christ reconciling the world to Himself" (2 Corinthians 5:19).

> *Archēgos*: This interesting Greek word is applied to Jesus several times in the New Testament, translated "prince" in Acts 3:15 and 5:31; "captain" in Hebrews 2:10 and "author" in 12:2.

How did Jesus *"taste death for everyone"* (2:9)? The answer is set out in the remaining verses of this chapter. The Lord Jesus Christ

could be the Saviour of mankind only by being made like his fellows; God accepted him as the representative of our sinful race:

> *"For both he who sanctifies and those who are being sanctified are all of one ... He is not ashamed to call them brethren ... Inasmuch then as the children have partaken of flesh and blood, he himself likewise shared in the same ... He had to be made like his brethren."*
> (2:11-17)

Phrase is piled upon phrase to emphasise that Jesus was a Son of man, of our nature, wholly identified with those he came to save. Three quotations (Psalm 22:22; 2 Samuel 22:3 and Isaiah 8:18) are used to prove that the Redeemer shared the nature of those whom he redeemed.

"BRINGING MANY SONS TO GLORY"

What a lot is contained in these five words! They eloquently summarise the eternal purpose of God manifestation and Christ's work of redemption: Jesus came for the very purpose of bringing "many sons to glory". The phrase echoes similar statements in other books of the New Testament:

- "The glory which You gave me I have given them" (John 17:22).
- "... joint heirs with Christ, if indeed we suffer with him, that we may also be glorified together" (Romans 8:17).
- "... that he might present her to himself a glorious church" (Ephesians 5:27).
- "... who will transform our lowly body that it may be conformed to his glorious body" (Philippians 3:21).
- "... when he comes, in that Day, to be glorified in his saints" (2 Thessalonians 1:10).

The words from Psalm 22 are especially poignant, for they follow on from the Psalmist's inspired description of the crucifixion:

"They pierced my hands and my feet ... they divide my garments among them ... But You, O LORD, do not be far from me; O my Strength, hasten to help me!"

Then, just before the verse quoted in Hebrews 2, comes the cry of the dying Saviour: "You have answered me" (22:16-21). The perceptive reader will have appreciated the relevance of the Psalm to the context.

ECHOES OF JOHN 17

In Hebrews 2:11-13, the inspired writer echoes phrases in Jesus' prayer for his disciples. Thus "he who sanctifies and those who are being sanctified are all of one" takes us to John 17:19-23 – "For their sakes I **sanctify** myself, that they also may be **sanctified** by the truth ... **that they may be one**". In addition, the phrase, "Here am I and the children whom God has given me", a quotation from Isaiah 8:18, is at the same time a lovely echo of John 17:6 – "I have manifested Your name to **the men whom You have given me** out of the world".

Jesus, a mortal man, yet sinless, was able to achieve what no other man could do, that is, to *"destroy him who had the power of death, that is,* **the devil**, *and release those who through fear of death were all their lifetime subject to bondage"* (2:14,15). The word "devil" presents no difficulty: we only need to turn to chapter 9 where the same truth is stated, but using the word "sin" instead of "devil": "Christ ... once at the end of the ages, has **put away sin** by the sacrifice of himself" (9:26).

Verse 16 may seem puzzling. The KJV translation is:

"For verily he took not on him the nature of angels; but he took on him the seed of Abraham."

This statement is in line with the many other statements about Jesus bearing the same nature as all mankind: if Jesus had come with angelic nature, he could never have redeemed mankind. However, the NKJV reads differently and makes a separate and valid point:

"He does not give aid to angels, but he does give aid to the seed of Abraham."

In other words, Jesus did not come to save angels but men and women.

And then, perhaps unexpectedly, Paul introduces the subject of priesthood – a theme that will occupy us for the next eight chapters:

"He had to be made like his brethren, that he might be a merciful and faithful High Priest ... to make propitiation for the sins of the people." (2:17)

In fact, priesthood follows on naturally from what has been said about Christ's nature. We have a high priest who shared our nature, and who therefore "can have compassion on those who are ... going astray, since he himself is also subject to weakness" (5:2). He can represent us in the presence of his Father.

Summarising chapters 1 and 2, we can say that Jesus, made in the image of God, yet sent as Son of man, for a little time lower than the angels, made like us, was able to save those of the human race who believe and turn to God through him. He resisted temptation, tasted death, and conquered sin:

"For in that he himself has suffered, being tempted, he is able to aid those who are tempted." (2:18)

POINTS TO PONDER

1. We are not tempted to keep to the Law of Moses, but what other things in the present world may cause us to drift from the truth?

2. Explain in your own words why Jesus, in order to be a Saviour, had to suffer and die.

3. How would you define "glory", as in "bringing many sons to glory"?

Hebrews chapter 3

"WORTHY OF MORE GLORY THAN MOSES"

THE writer has not so far addressed his readers directly; now he speaks to them:

"Therefore, holy brethren, partakers of the heavenly calling, consider the Apostle and High Priest of our confession, Christ Jesus, who was faithful to Him who appointed him, as Moses also was faithful in all his house. For this One has been counted worthy of more glory than Moses, inasmuch as he who built the house has more honour than the house."

(3:1-3)

"Brethren" is a very Jewish form of address. "Men and brethren" or "Brethren and fathers" is how the apostles introduced their speeches, or (in the case of Stephen and Paul) their defence before the authorities. *"Holy brethren"* is, however, almost unique to Hebrews – and it follows directly from what was said in the previous chapter (2:11), where those who are called the "brethren" of Jesus are "sanctified" (made holy). They are saints, *"partakers of the heavenly calling"* (in verse 14, *"partakers of Christ"*). And though Paul is desperately concerned that his readers seem reluctant to leave their old ways behind, at this stage he gives them the benefit of the doubt – these brethren had, after all, accepted the call of the Gospel and been baptized.

The phrases below show what a powerful train of thought is built up around the word "partake" and "partakers" in Hebrews.

- "Inasmuch then as the children have **partaken** of flesh and blood, he himself likewise **shared in** [partook of] the same" (2:14).
- "Therefore, holy brethren, **partakers** of the heavenly calling ..." (3:1).
- "We have become **partakers** of Christ if ..." (3:14).
- "... **partakers** of the Holy Spirit ..." (6:4).
- "... **partakers** of chastening ... that we may be **partakers** of his holiness" (12:8,10).

Apostle and High Priest

These holy brethren are invited to *"consider the Apostle and High Priest of our confession, Christ Jesus"*. They had once made a "confession", a profession of faith; and twice in later chapters they are exhorted: "Let us hold fast our confession" (4:14; 10:23). The Greek

"SPEAKING THE SAME THING"

- "All the people answered [Moses] **with one voice** and said, All the words which the LORD has said we will do" (Exodus 24:3).

- "... that you may **with one mind and one mouth** glorify the God and Father of our Lord Jesus Christ" (Romans 15:6).

word for "confession" is *homologia*, meaning 'speaking the same thing', and the challenge to the Hebrews was whether or not they were still believing and speaking the things they had confessed at their baptism. Throughout the ages, God has asked that, so far as the essentials of the faith are concerned, His people should be of one mind and speak with one voice.

In chapters 1 and 2, the Hebrews were asked to consider Jesus as Son of God and Son of man; now they are invited to consider him as Apostle and High Priest. Jesus had been compared with angels; now he is compared with Moses, in chapter 4 with Joshua, and in chapter 5 with Aaron. Moses, the man sent to speak to Pharaoh on behalf of Israel, was an Apostle ('one sent'), while Aaron was the first High Priest. In their respective roles, Moses and Aaron pointed forward to a greater Apostle and High Priest, Jesus Christ.

Jesus was the last in a succession of spokesmen sent by God. In that sense he was an apostle. Like Moses, he was sent by God to represent **God to man**; he was, in other words, a mediator. Remember how the people, trembling at the foot of Sinai, pleaded with Moses: "You speak with us, and we will hear; but let not God speak with us, lest we die" (Exodus 20:19). In agreeing to the people's request, Moses was inspired to foretell the coming of the Prophet like himself: "The LORD your God will raise up for you a Prophet like me from your midst, from your brethren. Him you shall hear ... he shall speak

to them all that I command him" (Deuteronomy 18:15-18). Jesus, the one of whom Moses was a type, was **sent** into the world to mediate God's new covenant with man. (Note incidentally how the verses from Deuteronomy confirm, yet again, that Jesus had to share the nature of his brethren – "from your midst, from your brethren".)

- "I will **send** them prophets and apostles, and some of them they will kill and persecute" (Luke 11:49).

- "Last of all he **sent** his son to them" (Matthew 21:37).

- "For God did not **send** His Son into the world to condemn the world, but that the world through him might be saved" (John 3:17).

A High Priest had a different role: he represented **man to God**. Though, in patriarchal times, there had been a tradition that the head of a household should have a priestly function (see Job 1:5), Aaron and his descendants were the first to be officially appointed, under the Law of Moses, to such a role. Jesus, though not of the order of Aaron (as later chapters will explain), has been appointed by God as a High Priest for ever.

Better than Moses

Jesus *"was faithful to Him who appointed him ... counted worthy of more glory than Moses, inasmuch as he who built the house has more honour than the house"* (3:2,3). Did the Hebrews not see that Moses, mighty and meek though he was, had now been succeeded by a better mediator?

> "For the law was given through Moses, but grace and truth came through Jesus Christ." (John 1:17)
>
> "Moses did not give you the bread from heaven, but my Father gives you the true bread from heaven ... I am the bread of life." (John 6:32-35)

Moses the lawgiver was a man all Jews revered; he was indeed *"faithful in all [God's] house"* (3:2; Numbers 12:7). But whereas Moses was *"faithful in all his house as a **servant** ... Christ [was faithful] as a **Son** over his own house"* (3:5,6). The writer is careful to give Moses due credit for his faithfulness, even though Moses was lower in rank than Jesus. Moses' faithful life and words were a *"testimony"* of things to be revealed later; he was a type of Christ.

> In verse 5, the word for "servant" is not the usual New Testament word for bondslave (*doulos*). It is a unique word (*therapōn*), occurring only here and meaning 'a willing and trusted household attendant'.

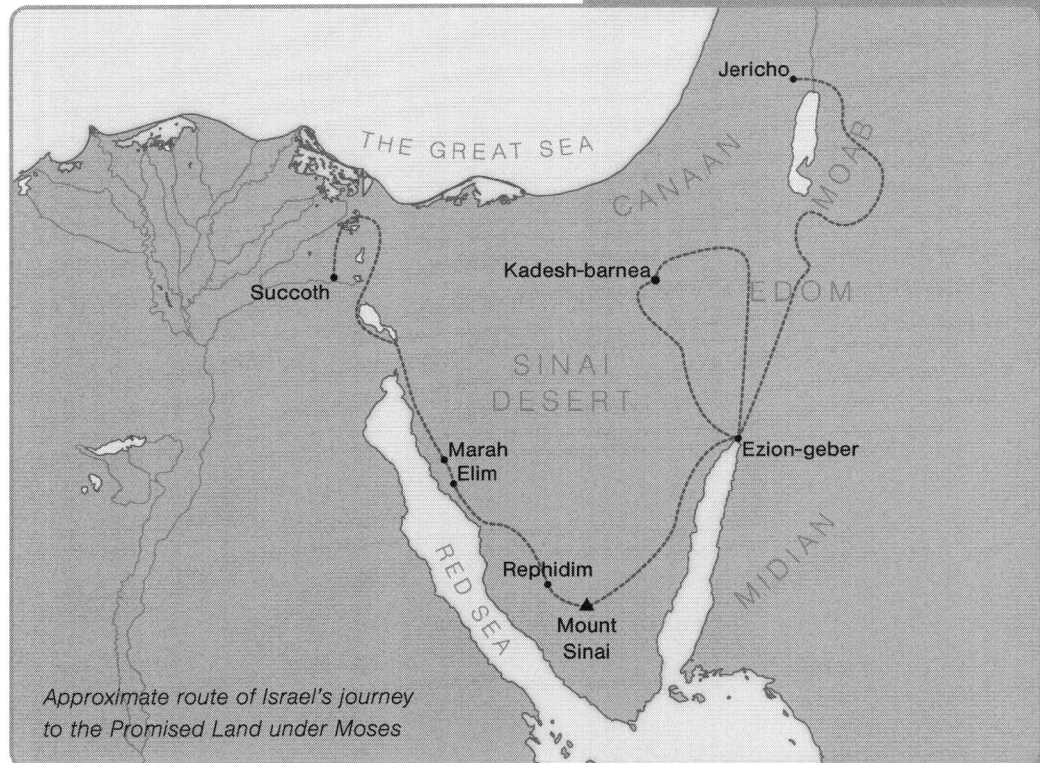

Approximate route of Israel's journey to the Promised Land under Moses

And, as if anticipating their question, 'What is Christ's house?' Paul adds, *"whose house **we** are"*; but then with a condition attached: *"if we hold fast the confidence and the rejoicing of the hope firm to the end"* (in verse 14, *"if we hold the beginning of our confidence steadfast to the end"*). Elsewhere Paul speaks about "the household of God ... built on the foundation of the apostles and prophets,

Jesus Christ himself being the chief cornerstone ... a holy temple in the Lord" (Ephesians 2:19-21). The apostle is clearly worried that the Hebrews were not holding fast to their confidence, and no longer rejoicing in their hope.

Massah and Meribah

So long as they resisted the call to let go of Moses, the Hebrews were demonstrating an attitude referred to in scripture as "hardness of heart", and the writer now reminds them (in the words of Psalm 95) of the consequences for Israel when they were rebellious: *"Today, if you will hear His voice, do not harden your hearts as in the rebellion, in the day of trial in the wilderness, where your fathers tested Me, tried Me, and saw My works forty years ... So I swore in My wrath, They shall not enter My rest"* (Hebrews 3:7-11, quoting Psalm 95:7-11).

Paul emphasises by his phrase *"as the Holy Spirit says"* (3:7) that Psalm 95 is inspired. The verses that he quotes are God's reminder to each new generation that it is always **today**; for the Hebrews, and for us, the opportunity is **now**!

The readers of this epistle would know that, in Psalm 95:8, the Hebrew words for "rebellion" and "trial" are in fact the place names Meribah and Massah, taking them back to the two occasions when Moses, in response to the people's rebellious complaining, miraculously provided water from a rock. There is much to learn from a comparison of the two incidents:

At Rephidim	At Kadesh
At the start of the wilderness wanderings, Moses with his own rod, struck the rock (*tzur*, a boulder), as God had commanded, and water came forth. "So Moses called the name of the place Massah (temptation) and Meribah (contention), because of the contention of the children of Israel, and because they tempted the LORD" (Exodus 17:1-7).	Forty years later, Moses, now with Aaron's rod, taken from "before the LORD" (Numbers 20:9; 17:10), was commanded only to speak to the rock (*selah*, a cliff or crag); instead he struck the rock twice.
The rod that Moses used to strike the rock was the one he used during the exodus and the journey to the promised land. The water that came forth lasted for a limited time: it reminds us of what Jesus said to the woman of Samaria: "Whoever drinks of this water will thirst again" (John 4:13).	Aaron's rod that budded symbolised resurrection and pointed forward to Christ, the source of living water. The water was (symbolically) from "the Rock that followed them". To strike this rock, instead of speaking to it, was (in a sense) to "crucify again the Son of God" (Hebrews 6:6). For his disobedience Moses was denied entry into the Land.
This water helped to bring Israel into their **temporary** rest – a rest achieved, as it were, through **works** of the Law.	Living water, offering the prospect of **eternal** rest, is obtained by **faith** – Moses, if he had had faith, could have brought forth water by speaking to the rock.

Rest

From 3:7 to 4:11, Paul expounds the reassuring theme of "rest", one which goes back to creation and the institution of the sabbath: "Then God blessed the seventh day and sanctified it, because in it He rested from all His work" (Genesis 2:3; Exodus 20:11). The weekly rest, the sabbath, prefigured a more lasting period of rest, and the theme begins to unfold as we see Israel being led towards the promised land – into their rest. On the border of the land, Moses told the people: "As yet you have not come to the rest ... but when you cross over the Jordan and dwell in the land which the LORD your God is giving you to inherit, and He gives you rest ..." (Deuteronomy 12:9,10).

> "Remember the word which Moses the servant of the LORD commanded you, saying, The LORD your God is giving you rest and is giving you this land."
>
> (Joshua 1:13)

This is the rest referred to in Psalm 95 – a rest which most of Israel never enjoyed because *"they always go astray in their heart, and they have not known My ways"*. But theirs was not the only generation guilty of unbelief. To the Hebrews Paul now says: *"Beware, brethren, lest there be in any of **you** an evil heart of unbelief in departing from the living God"* (3:12).

Four times in the Letter (3:12; 9:14; 10:31; 12:22) the Almighty is referred to as "the living God", a God to be served and worshipped, yet at the same time a Judge who will not overlook evil. How, then, could these brethren possibly contemplate "departing from the living God"? The Hebrews were to *"exhort one another daily, while it is called 'Today', lest any of you be hardened through the deceitfulness of sin"* (3:13). Many in Israel, including Moses himself, failed to enter that rest. But the consequence for those who turn their backs on Christ is so much

more serious: they will be excluded from God's **eternal** rest.

"For who, having heard, rebelled? ... With whom was he angry forty years? ... To whom did He swear that they would not enter His rest?" (3:16-18; Numbers 14:26-35). The answer to all three questions is the same: the unbelieving, faithless Israelites: *"So we see that they could not enter* [into that rest] *because of unbelief"* (3:19).

The Hebrews are warned not to repeat their fathers' mistake. They – and we – should not risk losing the prospect of eternal rest in the kingdom of God's Son.

POINTS TO PONDER

1. In what ways was Moses a 'type' of Christ?

2. What Old Testament passages suggest that the Christ would be (a) an Apostle; (b) a High Priest?

3. How often did the children of Israel put God to the test with rebellious words? (Numbers 14 is the clue).

4. In what sense is the kingdom to be a time of rest?

> "Our fathers ... all ate the same spiritual food, and all drank the same spiritual drink. For they drank of that spiritual Rock that followed them, and that Rock was Christ."
>
> (1 Corinthians 10:1-4)

Hebrews chapter 4

"LET US BE DILIGENT TO ENTER THAT REST"

"Let us" becomes a recurring phrase in Hebrews – always encouraging serious reflection and action.

THE theme of rest continues, but now the writer applies the lessons of chapter 3 to the Hebrews, concerned that they, like Israel leaving Egypt, might fail to reach their promised rest. For forty years Israel grieved God in the wilderness, and it would be tragic if now, nearly forty years after the death of Christ, believers should fall short as their fathers had done: *"Since a promise remains of entering his rest, let us fear lest any of you seem to have come short of it"* (4:1).

In verse 2 he goes on likening the generation of first century believers to those of earlier times, saying something which, at first sight, may be puzzling: *"For indeed the gospel was preached to us as well as to them."* "Gospel" means 'good news', and we associate it with the teaching of Jesus; so how was it "preached to them", that is, to Israel in the time of Moses? The good news of salvation and of the kingdom was indeed, in a very real sense, made plain to the patriarchs and the nation of Israel – see quotation alongside.

What God wanted of Israel was faith in the 'good news' which Moses constantly tried to teach them, *"but the word which they heard did not profit them, not being mixed with faith in those who heard it"* (4:2). This is the first time

we encounter "faith" in Hebrews, a topic that will build up to a climax in chapter 11. Faith is an essential attribute in those who would enter God's rest: *"For we who have **believed** [have faith] do enter that rest"* (4:3).

The Hebrews needed to refresh their understanding of God's rest. Being familiar with the account of creation in Genesis, they would accept that *"God rested on the seventh day from all his works"* (4:4; Genesis 2:2); but they must also see that His work has continued unceasingly ever since (John 5:17), leading always towards a final rest. God's *"works were finished from the foundation of the world"* in the sense that God could foresee from the beginning the outworking of His plan for the ages; but only in the kingdom, at the conclusion of the ages, would that rest finally be achieved.

With repeated reference to Psalm 95, Paul drives home the reality of that ultimate Day of rest. Obviously *"it remains that some must enter it"*. Israel's history was marked by lack of faith in every generation: *"Those to whom it [the Gospel] was first preached did not enter [the land] because of disobedience"* (4:6). Like their forefathers, Jews in the time of Christ and the apostles were slow to believe in the kingdom-rest

"The Scripture, foreseeing that God would justify the Gentiles by faith, **preached the Gospel to Abraham** beforehand." (Galatians 3:8)

which Jesus taught; they thought no further than the rest into which Israel entered under Joshua. But that was not the eternal rest that God intended: *"If Joshua had given them rest, then he would not afterward have spoken of another day"* (4:8). The very fact that the Psalmist, *"after such a long time"* (4:7), was still warning of failure to attain that rest, shows that the promise of true rest remained to be fulfilled. The "rest" under Joshua was a foretaste, a type, of the eternal "rest" to come.

"There remains therefore a rest"

So far in chapters 3 and 4, the Greek word Paul uses for "rest" has been *katapausis*, a word almost unique to Hebrews; it is used in one other place in the New Testament – significantly, in Stephen's speech (Acts 7:49). Suddenly, however, in Hebrews 4:9, Paul coins a **new** word, *sabbatismos*: *"There remains therefore a rest* [ESV, "a Sabbath rest"] *for the people of God."* By changing to a word associated with the sabbath, Paul emphasises the principle that, from creation onwards, God has had an eternal sabbath, an unending rest in view. The believer *"who has entered His* [God's] *rest has himself also ceased from his works as God did from His"* (4:10).

> "Blessed are the dead who die in the Lord ... that they may **rest** from their labours."
> (Revelation 14:13)

WHAT IS A 'TYPE'?

At a number of places in this Study Guide we refer to 'types'. The word does not occur in the King James Version of the Bible, but the idea does. A 'type' can be a person, object or event in the Old Testament that foreshadows something in the New Testament, or even an event yet to come. Thus, Joshua, the saviour of Israel, the one who brought God's people into the promised land, is a 'type' of Jesus, who came to save his people from death and bring them, ultimately, into his kingdom.

The exodus of Israel from Egypt prefigures the separation of the Christian believer from the world of darkness. The manna provided in the wilderness was a 'type' of the "true bread from heaven ... who gives life to the world" (John 6:32,33). As we shall see when we come to chapter 9, many aspects of the tabernacle and the Law were 'types' of things to come: for example, the High Priest entering the Holy of Holies was a 'type' of the risen Lord Jesus entering the presence of God.

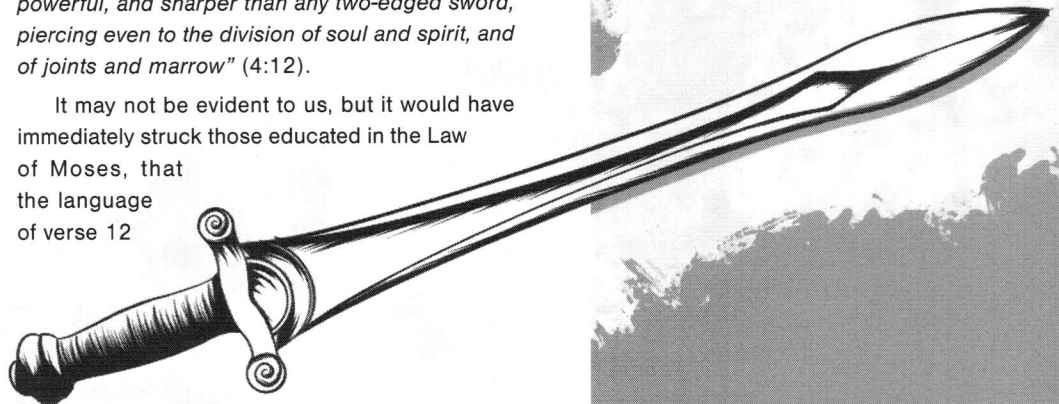

The final rest will be the culmination of the Father's gracious plan of salvation, and is not to be treated lightly: *"Let us therefore be diligent to enter that rest"* (4:11). God's word is not to be ignored: *"For the word of God is living and powerful, and sharper than any two-edged sword, piercing even to the division of soul and spirit, and of joints and marrow"* (4:12).

It may not be evident to us, but it would have immediately struck those educated in the Law of Moses, that the language of verse 12

> "He had in his right hand seven stars, out of his mouth went a sharp two-edged sword and his countenance was like the sun shining in its strength."
>
> (Revelation 1:16)

has to do with the ritual examination of a sacrificial animal for blemishes. The priest had to kill the animal and then open it up for inspection. Such vivic imagery must surely have had an effect on the Hebrews, particularly those who had themselves been priests with hands-on experience of the sacrifices.

We, with them, must be ready for the searching examination of the One before whose eyes *"all things are naked and open"*. And our High Priest is not looking for physical defects but, as the Word made flesh, is *"a discerner of the thoughts and intents of the heart"* (4:12,13).

"A great High Priest"

After demonstrating that Jesus was superior to angels, and greater than Moses and Joshua, the writer returns to his central theme of priesthood. The point was made in chapter 2 that in order to be a merciful and faithful high priest, Jesus had to be made like his brethren (2:14-18). Now, building on the fact that *"we have a great High Priest who is passed through the heavens, Jesus the Son of God"*, Paul exhorts his readers to *"hold fast our confession"* (same word as in 3:1). We have a sympathetic high priest, *"in all points tempted as we are, yet without sin. Let us therefore come boldly to the throne of grace, that we may obtain mercy and find grace to help in time of need"* (4:14-16).

Israel's prayers and worship arose symbolically to God with the "sweet savour" of the sacrifices and the incense burned daily on the incense altar by the priests. Once a year, on the Day of Atonement, the High Priest took burning incense into the Holiest – into the presence of God represented by the cloud above the mercy seat. Our great High Priest has "entered the Most Holy Place once for all ... into heaven itself, now to appear in the presence of God for us" (9:12,24). The exalted Lord Jesus intercedes in our prayers and worship before the Father's throne of grace.

"The throne of grace"

This is a unique phrase, found nowhere else in scripture, and it beautifully describes Christ's work of mediation and intercession at God's right hand. At that throne of grace, we can be

---

OUR HIGH PRIEST IN HEAVEN

- "A great High Priest who has passed through the **heavens**" (4:14).

- "A High Priest ... who ... has become higher than the **heavens**" (7:26).

- "We have such a High Priest, who is seated at the right hand of the throne of the Majesty in the **heavens**" (8:1; cf. 1:3).

- "Christ has ... entered into **heaven** itself, now to appear in the presence of God for us" (9:24).

---

confident of finding both mercy and grace, two of the great attributes of God Himself. On Sinai, God passed before Moses and proclaimed: "The LORD, the LORD God, **merciful and gracious**, longsuffering, and abounding in goodness and truth, keeping **mercy** for thousands, forgiving iniquity and transgression and sin, by no means clearing the guilty ..." (Exodus 34:6,7; Psalm 103:8). Bearing the Father's Name, Jesus manifests His attributes: "We beheld his glory, the glory as of the only begotten of the Father, full of **grace** and truth" (John 1:14).

"Mercy" has been roughly defined as 'not being judged as we deserve'; "grace" as 'being favoured more than we deserve'. These may not be dictionary definitions, but they are helpful as we approach God's throne, humbly acknowledging our need. Did the Hebrews acknowledge their need of mercy and grace? Perhaps not: it seems that they had been slow to develop their understanding of such spiritual qualities. The task of the author of Hebrews is to show that they are in desperate need of mercy and grace – which they will find in God's perfect High Priest, the Lord Jesus Christ.

POINTS TO PONDER

1. What aspects of the Gospel were preached to Abraham?

2. In what way was the Gospel preached to Israel, on their journey to the promised land?

3. The names Joshua and Jesus are the same (hence "Jesus" in Hebrews 4:8 in the KJV). How was Joshua a type of Jesus?

4. Does the expression "**throne** of grace" hint at the fact that Jesus is both priest and king?

5. How many times does "let us" occur in Hebrews?

Hebrews chapter 5

"THE AUTHOR OF ETERNAL SALVATION"

High priest of the order of Aaron

UNTIL the cataclysm of AD 70, worship continued in the temple in Jerusalem; the priests could be seen going about their duties; on the Day of Atonement, the High Priest still went into the Holy of Holies. For disciples of Christ in Jerusalem, the Law was everywhere: they were confronted daily with the sights and sounds and smells associated with the work of priests and Levites. Before delivering the Olivet Prophecy, Jesus, significantly, "went out and departed from the temple" (Matthew 24:1). But when would his followers have the courage to follow the same path and leave it all behind?

Those to whom the Letter to the Hebrews was addressed were evidently finding this separation difficult, and the writer faced a challenging task. In the end, he has to convince them that by the death of Jesus the Law had been superseded, and Christian converts had no place in the temple: that is what Paul will argue in the course of the next few chapters. But he builds up that argument gradually.

How should he approach the problem? He could have drawn his readers' attention to the corruption of the priesthood of the day and the many departures from the original laws of Sinai.

Jesus had been scathing in his comments: "Woe to you, scribes and Pharisees, hypocrites! For you pay tithe of mint and anise and cummin, and have neglected the weightier matters of the law ..." (Matthew 23:23). Paul had himself witnessed Stephen's outspoken denunciation: "You stiff-necked and uncircumcised in heart and ears! ... who have received the law by the direction of angels and have not kept it" (Acts 7:51-53). But Paul's readers were brothers and sisters; and in view of the fact that many had themselves once been priests or Levites, a direct attack on the priesthood and temple worship might not have been helpful.

The priesthood of Aaron

What happens in this and the next few chapters of Hebrews is that the writer, ignoring the present situation in Jerusalem, transports his readers back to the tabernacle in the wilderness, to the high priesthood of Aaron as it was originally intended, and in particular to the Day of Atonement. Instead of thinking in terms of Herod's temple, and the unfaithful shepherds who had brought about the death of Jesus, Paul (no doubt to the puzzlement of some of his readers) looked back to that earlier ideal:

CHAPTER 08

"For every high priest taken from among men is appointed for men in things pertaining to God, that he may offer both gifts and sacrifices for sins. He can have compassion on those who are ignorant and going astray, since he himself is also subject to weakness ... And no man takes this honour to himself, but he who is called by God, just as Aaron was." (5:1-4)

In this major section on the High Priesthood of Jesus Christ, which continues well into chapter 10, the Hebrews will be led calmly to reflect on the failure of the Levitical priesthood, contrasted with the perfection of the High Priest who was "according to the order of Melchizedek".

"The order of Melchizedek"

Disarmingly, Jesus is first introduced in 5:5 almost as if he were the natural successor to Aaron: he fulfilled the requirement that he should be compassionate, and he was "called by God, just as Aaron was". Thus far, there is nothing to cause offence or surprise.

But then Paul moves on to show that Jesus, far from being of Aaron's line, was a very special High Priest: he was God's Son. Psalm 2 has been quoted already in 1:5, and now the quotation is repeated: *"You are My Son, today I have begotten you"* (5:5; Psalm 2:7). Not only that, but Christ was High Priest of a more ancient order than Aaron. From the verse in Psalm 2 we are taken to Psalm 110 (also referred to in chapter 1)

where God declares concerning the Son ("my Lord") at His right hand: *"You are a priest forever according to the order of Melchizedek"* (5:6,10; Psalm 110:4).

Those who first listened to these words of the apostle being read to them must have held their breath. Why was the shadowy figure of Melchizedek being introduced? The reason was, of course, to show that, though God-given, Aaron's priesthood (and therefore the whole current system of law and worship) had proved ineffective. It was "imposed until the time of reformation" (9:10), and following the death and resurrection of Jesus it had been replaced by a more ancient – in fact, eternal – priesthood dating back to the time of Abraham.

> "The law was our tutor to bring us to Christ ... But after faith has come, we are no longer under a tutor." (Galatians 3:24,25)

Slowly, the writer is building his argument for the superiority of Christ's priesthood: over the course of the next few chapters, many more aspects of his priesthood will be noted, until finally that priesthood is confirmed as the "new and living way" which enables the believer himself to have "boldness to enter the Holiest by the blood of Jesus" (10:19,20).

Throughout chapters 5-7, Paul will keep returning to Melchizedek but, continuing in chapter 5, he now emphasises some very special attributes of Jesus which qualified him to be High Priest. We are invited to marvel at the humanity, the humility, the obedience, of the Son of man who –

> *"in the days of his flesh, when he had offered up prayers and supplications, with vehement cries and tears to Him who was able to save him from death, and was heard because of his godly fear, though he was a Son, yet he learned obedience by the things which he suffered."* (5:7,8)

Verse 7 echoes the experience of the Lord in the Garden of Gethsemane, where "he knelt down and prayed ... And being in an agony, he prayed more earnestly. Then his sweat became like great drops of blood falling down to the ground" (Luke 22:41-44). Our minds go also to the crucifixion, when, "at the ninth hour Jesus cried out with a loud voice, saying, Eloi, Eloi, lama sabachthani? which is translated, My God, my God, why have You forsaken me?" (Mark 15:34; cf. Psalm 22:1).

No High Priest had ever *"learned obedience by the things which he suffered"*, or come anywhere near the perfection of Jesus. Even the better High Priests, like Eleazar and Phinehas, the son and grandson of Aaron, or Joshua the son of Jehozadak after the return from exile, fell a long way short of the ideal. In any case, under the Law of Moses, no High Priest, however good, could offer salvation. Jesus, on the other hand,

> "My soul also is greatly troubled ... I am weary with my groaning ... The LORD has heard my supplication; the LORD will receive my prayer."
> (Psalm 6:3,6,9)

> "Save me from the lion's mouth and from the horns of the wild oxen! You have answered me ... When he cried to Him, he heard."
> (Psalm 22:21,24)

"having been perfected, became the author of eternal salvation to all who obey him" (5:9).

Milk and solid food

Could the confused Hebrews take all this in? An argument that began in 5:1 with an innocent reflection on the qualifications of Aaron, was now challenging their understanding. They had once been taught the Gospel, but had they ever heard such an exposition of the Psalm references, or of the priesthood of Melchizedek – *"of whom we have much to say, and hard to explain, since you have become dull of hearing"* (5:11)?

At this point, Paul becomes a bit more severe with his readers. He had started gently, but now begins to put on the pressure: *"For though by this time you ought to be teachers, you need someone to teach you again the first principles of the oracles of God; and you have come to need milk and not solid food"* (5:12).

> "I fed you with milk and not with solid food; for until now you were not able to receive it, and even now you are still not able."
> (1 Corinthians 3:2)

The use of the word *"again"* suggests that the Hebrews had once been taught those principles, but they had let them slip. And how ironic it was that those who once, as priests, had been teachers themselves now needed to be taught.

We are reminded of Nicodemus, to whom Jesus said: "Are you the teacher of Israel, and do not know these things?" (John 3:10).

The Hebrews were accused of being *"unskilled in the word of righteousness"*; they were spiritual babes, not yet ready for *"solid food [which] belongs to those who are of full age ... who by reason of use have their senses exercised to discern both good and evil"* (5:13,14). These were searching accusations, and chapter 6 will include more hard-hitting words – yet always tempered with compassion.

POINTS TO PONDER

1. Some of the Hebrews had been priests. What duties would they have performed in the temple?

2. What sustained the Lord Jesus during his agony in Gethsemane?

3. What aspects of the Gospel would Paul have considered as "milk" and what would be "solid food"?

Hebrews chapter 6

"LET US GO ON TO PERFECTION"

AT the end of chapter 5, the writer was telling the Hebrews: *"You need someone to teach you again the first principles of the oracles of God."* Now, at the start of chapter 6, he appears to contradict this: *"Therefore, **leaving** the discussion of the elementary principles of Christ, let us go on to perfection."* (Incidentally, "elementary" does not mean 'simple' but 'fundamental'.)

But there is no contradiction: Paul **does** want them to move on, *"not laying again the foundation ..."* Perhaps the sense of the opening words of chapter 6 is this: 'Even though you actually need to refresh your understanding of the basic principles of the Gospel of Christ, we must move on and help you towards maturity.' But what do we make of the foundation doctrines which follow? The writer includes six elements in this foundation, and they seem to come in pairs:

- *repentance from dead works / faith toward God*
- *baptisms / laying on of hands*
- *resurrection of the dead / eternal judgment*

Some commentators suggest that these are foundation truths of the Jewish faith: after all, the Old Testament taught repentance from sin, and faith toward God; the Law involved washings, and the laying of the offerer's hands on the sacrifices; and Old Testament men of faith believed in resurrection and judgment. On the other hand, repentance, faith, baptism, laying on of hands, resurrection and judgment are all involved in the Christian faith too (though the plural word translated "baptisms" is not the usual word for baptism into Christ).

The difficulty is, however, that this short list of just six points hardly does justice to either

---

"PERFECTION"

Expressions (in **bold**) based on *teleios* ('perfect') and related words:

- "Be ye therefore **perfect**" (Matthew 5:48).
- "I have **finished** the work which you have given me to do" (John 17:4).
- "In understanding be **mature**" (1 Corinthians 14:20).
- "Put on love, which is the bond of **perfectness**" (Colossians 3:14).
- "... to make the captain of their salvation **perfect** through sufferings" (Hebrews 2:10).
- "And having been **perfected**, he became the author of eternal salvation" (Hebrews 5:9).
- "Solid food belongs to those who are **of full age**" (Hebrews 5:14).
- "If **perfection** were through the Levitical priesthood ..." (Hebrews 7:11).
- "For by one offering he has **perfected** forever those who are being sanctified" (Hebrews 10:14).
- "Jesus, the author and **finisher** of our faith" (Hebrews 12:2).
- "His love has been **perfected** in us" (1 John 4:12).

the Jewish faith or the Christian faith. Essential to the Jewish faith would be the covenants of promise and the coming of Messiah. Essential to the Christian faith would be the doctrine of redemption by the death of the obedient Son of God and the hope of his second coming (among other things). There must surely be something special about the selection of the six points. Are they a short list of those principles which **the Hebrews** saw as the basics of the Christian faith – the Gospel as seen from a legalistic **Jewish** perspective? If that is the situation, then indeed the Hebrews had not progressed from *"milk"* to *"solid food"* and they needed to *"have their senses exercised"* (5:12-14). They were missing the deeper things of Christ.

The Hebrews, even though they were *"once enlightened"*, had not appreciated the full implications of the doctrines listed above. For example, if they really understood the importance of "repentance from dead works" they should go further and turn away from the dead works of the Law. If they had truly grasped the importance of "faith toward God" they must accept that salvation is by faith, not through the continuance of temple services.

Blessings ... and warnings

The writer is determined not to continue "discussion of the elementary principles of Christ", but to move forward and remind his readers of the blessings of the Gospel. And now his warnings become really strong:

"For it is impossible for those who were once enlightened, and have tasted the heavenly gift, and have become partakers of the Holy Spirit, and have tasted the good word of God and the powers of the age to come, if they fall away, to renew them again to repentance, since they crucify again for themselves the Son of God, and put him to an open shame." (6:4-6)

Those who fall away not only bring loss and hurt on themselves; they also bring the Gospel into disrepute, putting the Son of God "to an open shame". The Hebrews had known the truth, but were vulnerable. They were, after all, relatively new converts, tender plants, to be nurtured gently and brought to full flower – so long as they steadily mature. And that is exactly the imagery behind the next two verses – imagery drawn from Genesis chapters 1-3.

"For the earth which drinks in the rain that often comes upon it, and bears herbs useful for those by whom it is cultivated, receives blessing from God; but if it bears thorns and briers, it is rejected and near to being cursed, whose end is to be burned." (6:7,8)

The question for the Hebrews is whether they will flourish and give glory to God, or bear thorns and be rejected.

The apostle has been giving stern warnings, but these are now tempered with words of kindly encouragement: *"But, beloved, we are confident of better things concerning you ... God is not unjust to forget your work and labour of love which*

"You visit the earth and water it ... You make it soft with showers, You bless its growth." (Psalm 65:9,10)

"If anyone does not abide in me, he is cast out ... and they gather them and throw them into the fire, and they are burned." (John 15:6) *you have shown toward His name, in that you have ministered to the saints, and do minister"* (6:9-12). He recognises their good works; in fact, he had himself benefited from their ministrations – see 10:34.

"The hope set before us"

"And we desire that each one of you show the same diligence to the full assurance of hope until the end" (6:11). He pleads with them not to give up; they are to hold fast to their hope; they are not to *"become sluggish* [same word as "dull" in 5:11], *but imitate those who through faith and patience inherit the promises"* (6:12). Who were those who *"through faith and patience inherit the promises"*? The answer will come in chapter 11, where we have a catalogue of great men and women who *"died in faith, not having received the promises, but having seen them afar off"* (11:13,39). The greatest example of all was, of course, Abraham.

PAUL'S TRIAD OF VIRTUES

Paul brings "faith", "hope" and "love" together in a number of his epistles, and this feature could even be seen as one of his characteristic 'signatures', another hint that he was the author of Hebrews:

- "Having been justified by **faith** ... [we] rejoice in **hope** of the glory of God ... the **love** of God has been poured out n our hearts" (Romans 5:1-5).

- "And now abide **faith**, **hope**, **love**, these three; but the greatest of these is love" (1 Corinthians 13:13).

- "After I heard of your **faith** in the Lord Jesus and your **love** for all the saints ... you may know what is the **hope** of his calling" (Ephesians 1:15-18).

- "We give thanks ... since we heard of your **faith** in Christ Jesus and of your **love** for all the saints; because of the **hope** which is laid up for you" (Colossians 1:4,5).

- " ... remembering without ceasing your work of **faith**, labour of **love**, and patience of **hope** in our Lord Jesus Christ" (1 Thessalonians 1:3).

- "God is not unjust to forget your ... labour of **love** ... to the full assurance of **hope** until the end, that you ... imitate those who through **faith** and patience inherit the promises" (Hebrews 6:10-12).

- "Let us draw near ... in full assurance of **faith** ... Let us hold fast the confession of our **hope** ... And let us consider one another in order to stir up **love** and good works" (Hebrews 10:22-24).

> "For the promise that he would be the heir of the world was not to Abraham or his seed through the law, but through the righteousness of faith ... Therefore it is of faith that it might be according to grace."
>
> (Romans 4:13-16)

"For when God made a promise to Abraham, because He could swear by no one greater, He swore by Himself, saying, 'Surely blessing I will bless you, and multiplying I will multiply you.' And so, after he had patiently endured, he obtained the promise."

(6:13-15; Genesis 22:16,17)

This is the promise of Genesis 22, a promise which was given **after** Abraham had patiently endured – **after** he had endured the sore trial of being asked to sacrifice the son of promise.

The Hebrews were happy to associate themselves with the promises to Abraham. For faithful Jews, the promises to the patriarchs were beyond dispute. The writer and his readers were thus on common ground. And, like any good instructor, Paul would start from that common ground and work towards things connected with Abraham that might not be so well accepted or understood – in particular, an ancient priesthood that the Hebrews may never have considered.

We know that the writer is anxious to resume his discussion of Melchizedek, so why does he continue to dwell on the promises to Abraham? Why are we told that the promise was *"confirmed by an oath"*? And why is it so necessary to emphasise *"the immutability of God's counsel"*? The Hebrews, who seemed to be wavering, needed to be reminded that God's promises are certain; God does not change; God cannot lie. The promise and the oath – *"two immutable things"* – should give them *"strong consolation"* and encouragement to hold fast, as the *"heirs of promise"* had done (6:16-18).

"Fled for refuge"

"We might have strong consolation, who have fled for refuge to lay hold of the hope set before us" (6:18). That, of course, is an image drawn from the instruction for a manslayer under the Law (Numbers 35:9-34; Joshua 20). Someone who had unintentionally killed another could find sanctuary from the avenger of blood in the nearest city of refuge; and he was allowed to stay

there until the death of the High Priest. So, once more, the writer is subtly leading their thoughts to the high priesthood of Christ – to him we flee for refuge from sin; in him we can "lay hold of the hope set before us". The Lord Jesus Christ is a High Priest who never dies and ministers for us eternally in God's presence.

What else was Paul possibly hinting at by recalling the city of refuge? Could he be casting **them** in the role of manslayers? Of course, those who caused the death of Jesus acted with intent, whereas the manslayer here is one who killed unintentionally. Nevertheless, the imagery might well cause the perceptive reader to reflect on that earlier reference to those who, by falling away, in effect *"crucify again for themselves the Son of God"* (6:6). They must ask themselves if, by forsaking the way of salvation in Christ, they were guilty of such a terrible deed.

"An anchor of the soul"

A second metaphor is then employed to illustrate the nature of the hope which should be theirs:

"This hope we have as an anchor of the soul, both sure and steadfast, and which enters the Presence behind the veil, where the forerunner has entered for us, even Jesus, having become High Priest forever according to the order of Melchizedek." (6:19,20)

By all accounts, the People of the Land were not very interested in the open sea; the word "anchor" does not occur in the Old Testament.

Christians adopted the anchor as a symbol of hope: it is found engraved on rings and tombstones.

NAUTICAL IDIOMS

A number of nautical metaphors can be found in Hebrews, not all of them as obvious as the anchor here in 6:19. Other possible nautical idioms are as follows:

- 2:1 – "drift away", as when a ship drifts past the harbour and is wrecked.

- 10:35 – "cast away", as if throwing ballast overboard.

- 10:38,39 – "draw back", applied to lowering a sail and slackening the course.

- 13:9 – "carried about", or being swept off course by a current.

Paul, however, had plenty of experience of sea travel: on the ill-fated voyage to Rome, the mariners set their hopes on the anchors thrown overboard to avoid drifting (Acts 27:29,30). The Hebrews were in peril of making shipwreck of their faith (cf. 1 Timothy 1:19) and needed a strong anchor – the hope set before them.

A helpful extension of the anchor metaphor has been suggested: "In times of storm or stress, a small boat, or sometimes a man, would put off from a ship, and enter the harbour carrying a line which was made fast to an anchor within the harbour, and the ship was thus pulled to safety. The small boat was the forerunner" (John Carter, *The Letter to the Hebrews*, 2nd edition, page 64).

Paul then applies this imagery, and pictures for us the *"forerunner"*. But instantly the metaphor changes, for our forerunner has gone ahead, entering *"the Presence behind the veil"* ["into the inner place behind the curtain", ESV]. Jesus has entered into the Holiest, into the very presence of God. Our hope is firmly anchored to the Lord Jesus Christ who is at God's right hand and will shortly return: "Christ ... has entered ... into heaven itself, now to appear in the presence of God for us ...To those who eagerly wait for him he will appear a second time" (9:24,28; cf. John 14:1,2).

Finally in verse 20 of this chapter, at the end of a long digression for the purpose of exhortation and warning, we are brought deftly back to Melchizedek. Towards the end of chapter 5, the writer had introduced Melchizedek, "of whom we have much to say" (5:11) – and now he is able to pick up the thread of his argument again.

POINTS TO PONDER

1. Try listing the fundamental doctrines of our faith in Christ, under (say) twelve headings.

2. Can you think of examples of men of God entering into oaths?

3. In what sense are we like those who "fled for refuge" in Old Testament times?

Hebrews chapter 7

"A PRIEST ACCORDING TO THE ORDER OF MELCHIZEDEK"

U P to this point in the Letter, Melchizedek has been mentioned three times (5:6; 5:10; 6:20), each time by way of a quotation from Psalm 110:4 – "You are a priest forever according to the order of Melchizedek". Psalm 110 is David's inspired vision of the kingship and priesthood of the Messiah. The first verse of the psalm introduces us to "the LORD" (Yahweh) and to "my Lord", the Messiah, exalted to sit at God's right hand. David's "Lord" will rule from Zion (verse 2) and his people will be willing subjects (verse 3). But this ruler will also be a priest (verse 4) – a fact of special significance for the writer of Hebrews.

Who was Melchizedek? Genesis 14 is the unique Old Testament source of information about this enigmatic character. We are taken back to the patriarchal age, to the time of Abram, when five cities in the Jordan valley rebelled against the Elamite king Chedorlaomer. The five kings, including the king of Sodom, went to battle with Chedorlaomer and three of his allies, who had the upper hand. Abram's nephew Lot was among those taken captive, but Abram and his men went to rescue him and recover the spoil. Abram was successful, and the grateful king of Sodom met him and offered a reward. That could have been the end of the story, but three significant verses follow in the record:

"Then Melchizedek king of Salem brought out bread and wine; he was the priest of God Most High. And he blessed him and said: 'Blessed be Abram of God Most High, possessor of heaven and earth; and blessed be God Most High, who has delivered your enemies into your hand.' And he gave him a tithe of all." (Genesis 14:18-20)

An ancient priestly order

Hebrews 7 looks back at the ancient "king of Salem, priest of the Most High God" and sees in him a clear foreshadowing of the Lord Jesus Christ:

"For this Melchizedek, king of Salem, priest of the Most High God, who met Abraham returning from the slaughter of the kings and blessed him, to whom also Abraham gave a tenth part of all, first being translated 'king of righteousness,' and then also king of Salem, meaning 'king of peace,' without father, without mother, without genealogy, having neither beginning of days nor end of life, but made like the Son of God, remains a priest continually." (7:1-3)

The writer is venturing into new territory: in the Gospels there is no suggestion that Jesus ever expounded the type of Melchizedek, nor is there any hint in Acts – unless, possibly, Stephen is thinking of this incident when in Acts 7:48 he refers to God as "the Most High", a title also found in Genesis 14. The writer of Hebrews presents his readers with a series of new and challenging lessons to be drawn from Melchizedek:

1. Melchizedek was both king and priest – *"king of Salem, priest of the Most High God"* (7:1) – the archetype of a line of priest-kings down the ages (see "King and priest" on page 52). Being both king and priest, he was undoubtedly superior to Aaron. Is there special significance in the reference to "the Most High God" (El Elyon)? Where this title of the Almighty is used (and it does not occur frequently), it is usually in connection with His exaltedness and the glory of His kingdom – see, for example, Deuteronomy 32:8; Psalm 46:4; Daniel 7:27. It is certainly appropriate here.

2. The Hebrews' attention is directed to the translation of the name *Melchi-zedek*, *"king of righteousness"*, and to his position as king of Salem, meaning *"king of peace"* (7:2). David was a king of righteousness, and Solomon was a king of peace, but Jesus Christ merited both titles. There is significance in the coupling of "righteousness" and "peace", and especially in this order. There must be righteousness **before** there can be true peace: "The work of righteousness will be peace" (Isaiah 32:17).

3. Melchizedek is *"without father, without mother, without genealogy, having neither beginning of days nor end of life"* (7:3). Priests who served under the Law of Moses had to be able to trace their ancestry back to Aaron, and it was unthinkable that someone without that lineage could be part of the priesthood. Melchizedek was of a priestly order not dependent on ancestry: he was not even of Israel, let alone of the tribe of Levi or of the sons of Aaron.

4. Melchizedek was *"made like the Son of God"*: this is a stunning statement. We speak of Bible types and antitypes, and it might seem that the Son of God came into the world to fulfil the type foreshadowed in Melchizedek. But it is actually the other way round: **Melchizedek was made in the mould of his successor**. As verse 13 says, **Jesus** is the One *"of whom these things* [about the Melchizedek priesthood] *are spoken"*.

All this is evident from the first three verses of Hebrews 7, but as the chapter continues, the writer (sometimes, under inspiration, reading between the lines!) gleans yet more from the Genesis record:

5. *"Now consider how great this man was, to whom even the patriarch Abraham gave a tenth of the spoils"* (7:4). Under the Law, as verse 5 explains, Israel (Abraham's descendants) gave tithes of their goods for the support of the Levites; and a tenth of this tithe was given to the priests, who received it

"Having been justified [made righteous] by faith, we have peace with God through our Lord Jesus Christ." (Romans 5:1)

on God's behalf – "the LORD's heave offering" (Numbers 18:21-28). But long before the Law of Moses, we find Abraham paying tithes to Melchizedek. From this curious fact Paul makes a typically rabbinical deduction: he suggests to his readers that Levi, *"in the loins of his father"*, *"paid tithes through Abraham, so to speak"* (7:9,10). And if Levi (as it were) paid tithes to Melchizedek, someone who was wholly outside the Law, then Melchizedek is clearly superior to Aaron (of the tribe of Levi).

6. *"Melchizedek ... blessed him who had the promises"* (7:6). For Jews, Abraham was their greatest ancestor, the father of the nation, the one to whom God gave the covenants of promise. Yet the devastating logic of Paul's reasoning is that there was, in fact, one greater. Melchizedek blessed Abraham, so Melchizedek is the greater of the two: *"Now beyond all contradiction the lesser is blessed by the better"* (7:7). And if Melchizedek was better than Abraham, then Jesus was greater still.

7. *"Here mortal men* [the Levitical priests] *receive tithes, but there he* [Melchizedek] *receives them, of whom it is witnessed that he lives* ['having neither beginning of days **nor end of life**']" (7:8). Once more, without attacking the temple priests, Paul is proving that they are of a lesser order than Melchizedek.

Paul still has not exhausted his arguments demonstrating the superiority of Melchizedek's – and therefore Christ's

– priesthood, and several more proofs are given in verses 11-21:

8. *"If perfection were through the Levitical priesthood ... what further need was there that another priest should rise ...?"* (7:11). The answer is that, alas, *"the law made nothing perfect"* (7:19), so that there has to be a change of priesthood – and *"also a change of the law"* (7:12).

9. *"He of whom these things are spoken belongs to another tribe ... our Lord arose from Judah, of which tribe Moses spoke nothing concerning priesthood"* (7:13,14). Shocking as it must have sounded to Jews brought up under the Law, there is nothing in God's eternal purpose that necessarily links priesthood with Levi, even though priests under the Law of Moses were from that tribe.

10. Unlike those mortal priests, Christ, arising *"in the likeness of Melchizedek"*, can claim

How little did the Jews understand when they asked Jesus the question: "Are you greater than our father Abraham, who is dead?" Nor did they understand his answer:

"Your father Abraham rejoiced to see my day, and he saw it and was glad ... before Abraham was, I am."   (John 8:53,56,58)

PRIESTS AND LEVITES IN NEW TESTAMENT TIMES

There were twenty-eight high priests between 37 BC and AD 70, with frequent changes as a result of intrigue and power struggles. Some high priests may have been able to trace their lineage from Aaron, but others, including some appointed by the Herods or even by Roman governors, were not legitimate successors.

Besides the High Priest(s) there were the 'chief priests' – the Captain of the Temple, the treasurers, the temple overseers, and leaders of the weekly and daily courses (cf. Acts 4:1,5; 5:22,24,26) – a hierarchy numbering nearly 200. Then there were more than 7,000 'ordinary' priests in their twenty-four weekly courses; and Levites numbering as many as 10,000.

"the power of an endless life"; he is "a priest forever" (7:15-17). Instead of "the former commandment", limited by its "weakness and unprofitableness", we have been offered "a better hope, through which we draw near to God" (7:18,19). And unlike that of Aaron, Christ's priesthood was conferred "with an oath": "The Lord has sworn and will not relent" (7:20,21; Psalm 110:4). As a result, "Jesus has become a surety [guarantee] of a better covenant" (7:22).

11. In Aaron's line "there were many priests, because they were prevented by death from continuing"; but the immortal Christ, "because he continues forever, has an unchangeable priesthood" (7:23,24).

12. Our High Priest excels because he "does not need daily, as those high priests, to offer up sacrifices, first for his own sins and then for the people's, for this he did once for all when he offered up himself. For the law appoints as high priests men who have weakness, but the word of the oath ... appoints the Son who has been perfected forever" (7:27,28). The contrast here is between "men" and "the Son": the Hebrews were trusting in men, and not appreciating the infinite superiority of Jesus, the Son of God.

We have left verses 25 and 26 until last, because they provide a masterly summary, not just of this chapter, but of earlier statements concerning the sinlessness and exaltation of the Saviour (compare 2:17,18; 4:14,15):

"Therefore he is also able to save to the uttermost those who come to God through him, since he always lives to make intercession for them. For such a High Priest was fitting for us, who is holy, harmless, undefiled, separate from sinners, and has become higher than the heavens." (7:25,26)

"He always lives to make intercession"

This is the only time "intercession" appears in Hebrews, and the only other place where the same word is used in relation to the work of Jesus is Romans 8 (verses 26,27,34). Hebrews 7:25 is a precious statement and should have been recognised as such by the recipients of this Letter. The writer will concentrate later on Jesus Christ as the "mediator of the new covenant" (8:6; 9:15; 12:24), but in 7:25 we have a specific reference to his continuing work as "intercessor" at God's right hand, bringing our prayers before his Father. Through the Lord Jesus Christ we can approach the throne of grace with boldness (4:16; 10:19-22).

> "It is Christ who died, and furthermore is also risen, who is even at the right hand of God, who also makes intercession for us."
> (Romans 8:34)

Aaronic High Priests wore "holy garments ... for glory and for beauty", and a plate on the forehead engraven with the words "HOLINESS TO THE LORD"; they were anointed with the

---

Phinehas, son of Eleazar, and grandson of Aaron was a faithful priest; indeed, he could be said to be worthy of the line of Melchizedek, for of Phinehas the Lord said:

"Behold, I give to him my **covenant of peace**; and it shall be to him and his descendants after him a **covenant of an everlasting priesthood**, because he was zealous for his God." (Numbers 25:12,13; see also Psalm 106:30,31)

holy anointing oil (Exodus 28:2,36; 30:30). Yet these were mere outward signs of consecration; they were not holy within. Only of God's true High Priest could it be said that he was "holy, harmless, undefiled, separate from sinners".

What next?

Surely, by the end of chapter 7, Paul has said enough to encourage the Hebrews to abandon the Law and move on to greater maturity in Christ. Paul has conclusively shown that the

---

KING AND PRIEST

In Israel of old, the roles of King and High Priest were distinct. Yet in the eternal purpose of God, kingship and priesthood do not have to be separate. In a number of places in the Old Testament, priesthood and kingship combine, providing types and prophecies of the coming Messiah:

- Melchizedek was both **king** of Salem, and **priest** of the Most High God (Genesis 14:18).

- Moses acted as a **ruler** in Israel and also, at times, as a **priest** (even though God had appointed Aaron and his sons to be the priests). Moses was executing a priestly function when he consecrated Aaron and his son (Exodus 29). Even more significantly, "When Moses went into the tabernacle of meeting [something only a priest should do] to speak with Him, he heard the voice of One speaking to him from above the mercy seat that was on the ark of the Testimony, from between the two cherubim" (Numbers 7:89).

- Israel was to be "a **kingdom of priests** and a holy nation" (Exodus 19:6).

- When **King** David brought up the ark of God to Jerusalem, he took on the function of a **priest**: "He sacrificed oxen and fatted sheep ... David was wearing a linen ephod ... And when David had finished offering burnt offerings and peace offerings, he blessed the people in the name of the LORD" (2 Samuel 6:12-18).

- Psalm 45 is a psalm "concerning the **king**" (verse 1); but **priesthood** is also hinted at in verses 7,8: "God has anointed you with the oil of gladness ... your garments are scented with myrrh and ... cassia" – two of the components of the holy anointing oil used for the consecration of the tabernacle and the High Priest (Exodus 30:22-33; cf. Psalm 133:2).

- "Behold, the Man whose name is the BRANCH! ... He shall build the temple of the LORD ... He shall bear the glory, and shall sit and rule on his throne; so he shall be a **priest** on his [**kingly**] throne" (Zechariah 6:12,13).

- The wise men "presented gifts to him: gold, frankincense, and myrrh" (Matthew 2:11) – gifts symbolic of **kingship** and **priesthood**.

In the kingdom, the saints are destined to be kings and priests:

- "You shall be named the **priests** of the LORD ... You shall also be a crown of glory in the hand of the LORD, and a **royal** diadem in the hand of your God" (Isaiah 61:6; 62:3).

- "You are a chosen generation, a **royal priesthood**, a holy nation, his own special people" (1 Peter 2:9).

- "Jesus Christ ... has made us **kings and priests** to his God and Father" (Revelation 1:5,6; 5:10).

- "They shall be **priests** of God and of Christ, and shall **reign** with him a thousand years" (Revelation 20:6).

risen Lord Jesus is the perfect High Priest, making the priesthood of Aaron and the Law of Moses redundant. So, could he not have finished at this point, perhaps rounding off with the 'faith chapter' (chapter 11), and the exhortations of chapters 12 and 13?

The answer is that the Hebrews might still need more to persuade them to move on. The apostle must prove that Jesus is not only a better High Priest, but that he redeemed us with a better sacrifice. In chapters 8-10, we now have Paul's unequalled exposition on the shedding of the blood of Christ for the remission of sins.

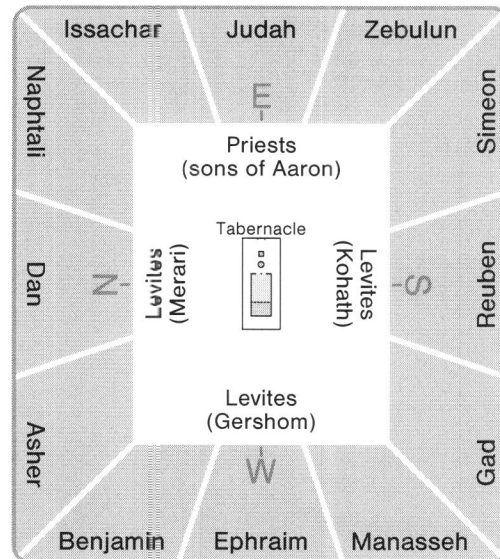

Tribes, priests and Levites around the tabernacle: In the encampment of the tribes of Israel, in the wilderness, the tribe of **Judah** *(the kingly tribe) was on the east of the tabernacle, as also were the priests. It is no coincidence that the representatives of kingship and priesthood should find themselves close together.*

POINTS TO PONDER

1. How is Melchizedek superior to Aaron?

2. In what ways is Christ, as King and Priest, superior to Melchizedek?

3. What tasks will the "kings and priests" of the future age perform?

4. What does '"intercession" mean, for those who pray to God?

5. List the occurrences of "once" and "once for all" (e.g., 7:27) in Hebrews.

Hebrews chapter 8

"MEDIATOR OF A BETTER COVENANT"

HEBREWS is, without doubt, the epistle of priesthood; in fact it is the only epistle which contains the actual word "priest" (or "high priest"). No other ecclesia had the Hebrews' problem – the need to sever themselves, finally, from the obsolete priesthood of the temple in Jerusalem and recognise the high priesthood of Christ.

That priesthood has been the focus of Hebrews from chapter 2 onwards:

- "In all things he had to be made like his brethren, that he might be a merciful and faithful High Priest" (2:17).

- He is "the apostle and High Priest of our confession" (3:1).

- "We have a great High Priest who ... was in all points tempted as we are, yet without sin" (4:14,15).

- "You are a priest forever according to the order of Melchizedek" (5:6 etc.).

- "Such a High Priest was fitting for us ... holy, harmless, undefiled ... higher than the heavens" (7:26).

Now, in chapter 8, the writer reviews the points made so far: *"This is the main point of the things we are saying ..."* (8:1). But the phrase "we are saying" implies that he has not finished; there is more to come – other aspects of Christ's work are to be discussed in chapters 8-10. Today's reader might well ask: 'Isn't Paul grinding too finely? Is he not getting too deep?' To us it may seem that the writer has already more than proved the superiority of the Lord's priesthood, but this is a large subject and his arguments must continue if the Hebrews are finally to be convinced. Verses 1 and 2 set the scene, then, for further exposition:

"We have such a High Priest, who is seated at the right hand of the throne of the Majesty in the heavens, a Minister of the sanctuary and of the true tabernacle which the Lord erected, and not man." (8:1,2)

"At the right hand of God"

Here is yet another echo of Psalm 110, where "the Lord" is commanded to "**sit** at my right hand". Notice how, five times in the Letter, Paul quotes this psalm to highlight the exalted position of the risen Christ at God's right hand:

- "He ... sat down at the right hand of the Majesty on high" (1:3).

- "To which of the angels has he ever said: Sit at My right hand ...?" (1:13).

- "[He] ... is seated at the right hand of the throne of the Majesty in the heavens" (8:1).

- "You will see the Son of Man sitting at the right hand of the Power, and coming on the clouds of heaven" (Matthew 26:64).
- "After the Lord had spoken to them, he was received up into heaven, and sat down at the right hand of God" (Mark 16:19).
- "... who is even at the right hand of God" (Romans 8:34).
- "... seated him at His right hand in the heavenly places" (Ephesians 1:20).
- "... where Christ is, sitting at the right hand of God" (Colossians 3:1).
- "... at the right hand of God, angels and authorities and powers having been made subject to him" (1 Peter 3:22).

"If I have told you earthly things and you do not believe, how will you believe if I tell you heavenly things?" (John 3:12)

- "This man, after he had offered one sacrifice for sins forever, sat down at the right hand of God" (10:12).
- "Jesus ... has sat down at the right hand of the throne of God" (12:2).

Aaron served in an earthly sanctuary, a man-made (though divinely designed) tabernacle; Jesus serves in a heavenly sanctuary, the true tabernacle. In the course of his priestly duties Aaron never sat (10:11) because his work was never finished; Jesus completed his sacrificial work and is worthy to sit at the Father's right hand.

Earthly and heavenly things

Constantly, in these middle chapters of Hebrews, the writer is seeking to convince his readers of the superior nature of the priesthood of Christ. How can they possibly think of continuing with the Law, the temple, and the offerings, when all had been fulfilled in the death and resurrection of Jesus? From chapter 7 onwards, in fact until the end of the Letter, he repeatedly contrasts the old and the new, the earthly and the heavenly, Aaron and Jesus. In the following chart, aspects of the old order are compared with the new in Christ:

Ref.	The old	The new
7:11	"the Levitical priesthood"	"priest ... according to the order of Melchizedek"
7:14	Aaron was of the tribe of Levi	"our Lord arose from Judah"
7:16	"the law of a fleshly commandment"	"the power of an endless life"
7:19	"the law made nothing perfect"	"a better hope, through which we draw near to God"
7:21	"priests without an oath"	"but [Jesus] with an oath"
7:23,24	"many priests ... prevented by death from continuing"	"he, because he continues forever, has an unchangeable priesthood"
7:27	"daily ... high priests offer up sacrifices"	"this he did once ... when he offered up himself"

Ref.	The old	The new
7:28	"high priests .. who have weakness"	"the Son who has been perfected forever"
8:1	Aaronic High priests stood	"[Christ] ... seated at the right hand of [God]"
8:2; 9:11	A tabernacle which man erected	"the true tabernacle which the Lord erected"
8:5,6	"the copy and shadow of the heavenly things"	"a more excellent ministry"
8:13,6	"the first [covenant] ... obsolete"	"a better covenant ... established on better promises"
9:7,12	"into the [Holiest] the high priest went ... not without blood"	"Christ ... with his own blood entered the Most Holy Place"
9:13,14	"blood of bulls and goats ... sanctifies for the purifying of the flesh"	"the blood of Christ ... cleanse[s] your conscience"
9:23	"copies of things in the heavens ... purified with these [offerings]"	"heavenly things themselves with better sacrifices"
9:25,28	"the high priest enters ... every year"	"Christ was offered once"
10:1	"the law, having a shadow of the good things to come"	"[in Christ] the very image of the things"

We cannot fail to be amazed and moved by such comparisons! But were the Hebrews convinced that the new covenant is indeed better than the old; that the blood of Jesus is more effective than the blood of bulls and goats; that the high priesthood of Christ is superior in every way to that of the high priests functioning in the temple at that time? Every element of the Law of Moses had in fact been superseded.

Shadow and reality

In Jesus Christ everything has a heavenly perspective. The earthly ordinances of the Law of Moses have been replaced by the heavenly – of which those earthly arrangements were but a shadow: *"For if he [Jesus] were on **earth**, he would not be priest, since there are priests who offer the gifts according to the law; who serve the copy and shadow of the **heavenly** things"* (8:4,5). To some of the Hebrews to whom Paul was writing these were still perplexing issues: to them the Law and the Temple were real and solid, and they had to be educated to understand that the true reality was not to be found in those familiar sights and sounds of the Jerusalem they knew.

The language of shadows or copies is almost exclusively to be found in Hebrews, though there is one verse in Colossians (see alongside) which uses the same metaphor:

- "[Aaronic priests] *serve the **copy and shadow** of the **heavenly** things, as Moses was divinely instructed when he was about to make the tabernacle. For He said, See that you make all things according to the pattern shown you on the mountain"* (8:5; Exodus 25:40; 26:30; 27:8; see also Acts 7:44).

- *"Therefore it was necessary that the **copies** of the things in the heavens should be*

purified with these, but the **heavenly things themselves** with better sacrifices than these"* (9:23).

- *"The law, having a **shadow** of the good things to come, and not the **very image** of the things, can never ... make those who approach perfect"* (10:1).

We are not told what "pattern" Moses was shown in Mount Sinai, but it does seem that significant aspects of the tabernacle construction were revealed which the Exodus account (chapters 25-30) does not contain. Perhaps, in vision, Moses was granted some glimpse of the eternal heavenly sanctuary, of which the tabernacle and its institutions were but a shadow.

The new covenant

In chapter 7 it was stated that "Jesus has become a surety of a better covenant" (7:22). That statement is now developed further: *"But now he has obtained a more excellent ministry, inasmuch as he is also Mediator of a better covenant, which was established on better promises"* (8:6). The old covenant, at Sinai, was mediated by Moses (Exodus 24:7); the new covenant was mediated by one greater than Moses, and sealed by the blood of his own sacrifice. At the Last Supper, Jesus said, "This cup is the new covenant in my blood, which is shed for you" (Luke 22:20).

Hebrews 9 will take up this theme of the shedding of blood, but meanwhile chapter 8 refers us to Jeremiah's prophecy of the new covenant:

"Let no one judge you in food or in drink, or regarding a festival or a new moon or sabbaths, which are a **shadow** of things to come, but the **substance** is of Christ."
(Colossians 2:16,17)

"Behold, the days are coming, says the LORD, when I will make a new covenant ... this is the covenant that I will make with the house of Israel after those days, says the LORD: I will put My laws in their mind and write them on their hearts; and I will be their God, and they shall be My people ... For I will be merciful to their unrighteousness, and their sins and their lawless deeds I will remember no more."

(8:8-12; Jeremiah 31:31-34)

Sadly, the Law of Moses had never been written on Israel's heart, and it would in any case always fail to provide for the permanent forgiveness of sins. The new covenant, by contrast, provided a way of grace whereby sins could be blotted out for ever.

Better promises

The new covenant was a better covenant, moreover, because it was "established on better promises" (8:6). What particular promises did the writer have in mind? Within the Letter to the Hebrews we have several mentions of those promises:

- "A **promise** remains of entering His rest" (4:1).

- "Imitate those who through faith and patience inherit the **promises** ... God made a **promise** to Abraham ... after he had patiently endured, he obtained the **promise**" (6:12-15).

- "[Melchizedek] blessed him [Abraham] who had the **promises**" (7:6).

- "Those who are called may receive the **promise** of the eternal inheritance" (9:15).

- "You have need of endurance, so that after you have done the will of God, you may receive the **promise**" (10:36).

- "These all died in faith, not having received the **promises**, but having seen them afar off were assured of them ..." (11:13,39).

These refer, in the first place, to the promises to Abraham and his descendants of a land and a kingdom, but through the death of Jesus, the promised Seed, came also redemption and the promise of eternal life to those who would believe and be baptized in his name. These are truly "better promises" – promises in addition to those made to Abraham.

Jesus, by his death and resurrection, *"has made the first* [covenant] *obsolete.*

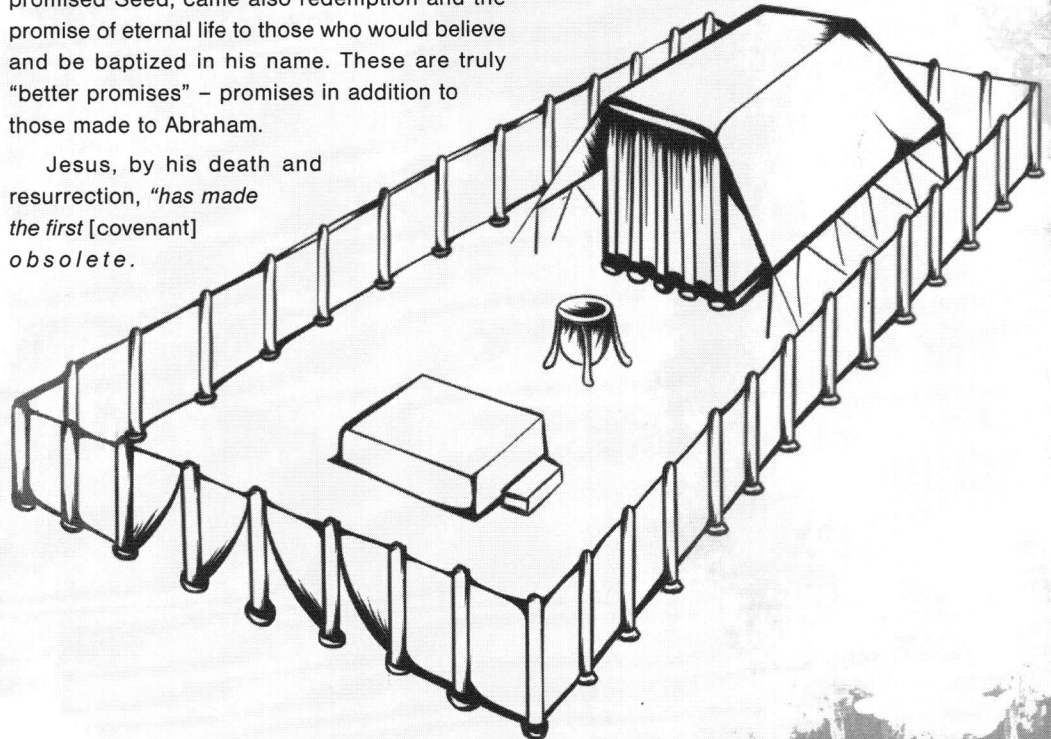

Now what is becoming obsolete and growing old is ready to vanish away" (8:13). Instead of letting it vanish away, however, the Hebrews appeared to want the old order to continue.

> "Therefore, if anyone is in Christ, he is a new creation; old things have passed away; behold, all things have become new."
> (2 Corinthians 5:17)

POINTS TO PONDER

1. Look up the passages in the Gospels and Acts where (a) Jesus, (b) Peter, and (c) Paul came face to face with the high priest(s) of the day. Were those high priests worthy of their office?

2. What is the difference between a mediator and an intercessor?

3. What has to happen before God can make "a new covenant with the house of Israel and with the house of Judah" (8:8)?

Hebrews chapter 9

"THE GREATER AND MORE PERFECT TABERNACLE"

THE old (or first) covenant, the covenant of Sinai, is "ready to vanish away": Jesus is the mediator of a new and better covenant. That was the message of chapter 8. Chapter 9 continues to explain how the new has superseded the old: *"Then indeed, even the first covenant had ordinances of divine service and the earthly sanctuary"* (9:1). The writer to the Hebrews takes his readers back to that "earthly sanctuary" – the tabernacle in the wilderness. And, by the way, as we read the description of those past arrangements, we should note that whilst Paul is seeking to demonstrate that **the new is better**, he always speaks reverentially of the old order.

Why does the writer base his arguments on the long-forgotten **tabernacle**, rather than the temple which Jews of the time knew so well? There are several possible reasons:

- They may be sensitive about their cherished place of worship – a place where many of them, as priests, had worked. The writer can be dispassionate about the tabernacle which, after all, belonged to a bygone era.

- Paul can subtly remind them that the tabernacle eventually ceased to be used; it became obsolete. He can move on from

there to point out that, in Christ, the **whole** of the Law has now been superseded.

- The tabernacle was not in Jerusalem but "in the wilderness", a further reminder that the worship of God was not necessarily associated with Jerusalem and the temple. (Stephen, in his speech, makes the same point: he too goes back to the "tabernacle of witness", and it is interesting that Stephen repeats the phrase "in the wilderness" five times, as part of his argument that God could be acceptably worshipped away from Jerusalem: see alongside.)

- Another reason for focusing on the tabernacle could be that the author's illustrations from the Law – for example, what happened on the Day of Atonement – are more powerful when they are related to the pristine tabernacle in the wilderness and the priesthood of Aaron, to the time when the ark still contained the tables of the covenant, the pot of manna and Aaron's rod (9:4), and before the rituals were embellished with later additions.

"The earthly sanctuary"

Though the tabernacle had long since disappeared, it still held lessons for those who would reflect upon its construction and contents:

"IN THE WILDERNESS" IN STEPHEN'S SPEECH

- "An angel of the Lord appeared to Moses ... **in the wilderness**" (Acts 7:30).

- "... wonders and signs ... **in the wilderness** forty years" (verse 36).

- "This is he who was in the congregation **in the wilderness**" (verse 38).

- "Did you offer Me ... sacrifices during forty years **in the wilderness**, O house of Israel?" (verse 42).

- "Our fathers had the tabernacle of witness **in the wilderness**" (verse 44).

THE TABERNACLE

- Strictly, the **tabernacle** (Hebrew: *mishkan*) was the inner one of four coverings, spread over wooden frames standing on metal sockets; it was made up of "ten curtains of fine woven linen, and blue, purple, and scarlet thread; with artistic designs of cherubim" (Exodus 26:1). The other coverings were of goat hair, ram skins and badger (or seal) skins.

- Entrance to the tabernacle was through a **Gate** into the **Outer Court**: only the serving priests and Levites could enter the Court; only the priests were allowed through a **Screen / Door** into the first section of the tabernacle, the **Holy Place**; while only the High Priest, once a year on the Day of Atonement, might enter through the **Veil** into the innermost shrine, the **Holy of Holies** (also known as the **Holiest** or the **Most Holy Place**). The veil was of the same materials and colours, and **woven** in the same way, as the inner tabernacle covering, with cherubim The gate and door hangings were of fine linen, **embroidered** with blue, purple and scarlet thread but without cherubim.

- The Court contained the bronze **Altar** and the **Laver**. In the Holy Place were the **Table of Showbread**, the **Lampstand**, and the **Altar of Incense**; while in the Holiest of all was the **Ark of the Covenant** (or Testimony) surmounted by the **Mercy Seat** and the **Cherubim** of glory overshadowing the mercy seat.

- Inside the ark were the **Golden pot of manna** that did not corrupt (symbolic of eternal life: John 6:51); **Aaron's rod that budded** (evidence of divine authority, as well as foreshadowing resurrection from the dead); and the stone **Tablets of the law** (God's enduring covenant with Israel).

The Exodus account does not actually refer to a **golden** pot of manna – at least in the Hebrew text. However, the Greek Septuagint inserts "golden" before "pot" in Exodus 16:33.

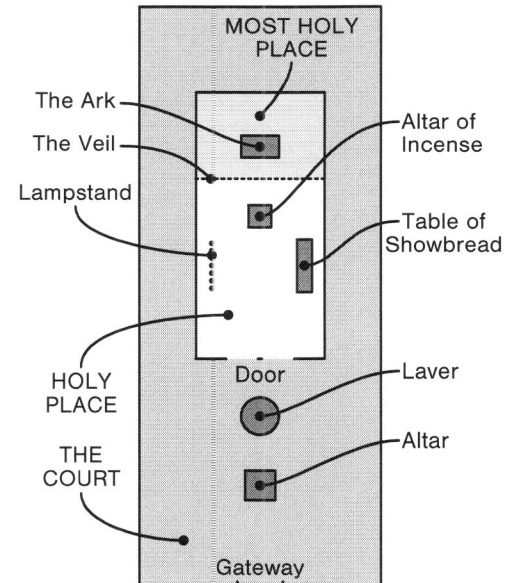

We cannot imagine that a pot, kept in the ark of the covenant in the Holy of Holies, would be made of anything other than gold.

"For a tabernacle was prepared:

the first part, in which was the lampstand, the table, and the showbread, which is called the sanctuary [the Holy Place];

and behind the second veil, the part of the tabernacle which is called the Holiest of All [the Holy of Holies], *which had the golden censer and the ark of the covenant overlaid on all sides with gold, in which were the golden pot that had the manna, Aaron's rod that budded, and the tablets of the covenant; and above it were the cherubim of glory overshadowing the mercy seat."* (9:2-5)

Compared with the temple of Solomon, or Herod's temple in the time of Jesus, the tabernacle in the wilderness was a modest sanctuary, small yet beautifully fashioned from the gifts of willing people, an edifice full of spiritual meaning. Like the writer to the Hebrews, *"we cannot now speak in detail"* about every aspect of the tabernacle, but its more significant features are summarised in the box, and illustrated in the diagram (the full specification of the tabernacle is detailed in Exodus 25-30).

Mercy seat and cherubim

The mercy seat was at the centre of Israel's worship – and most particularly on the Day of Atonement: "The LORD said to Moses: Tell Aaron your brother not to come at just any time into the [Most] Holy Place, inside the veil, before the mercy seat which is on the ark, lest he die; for I will appear in the cloud above the mercy seat" (Leviticus 16:2). On the Day of Atonement, the cloud of incense covered the mercy seat (shielding the High Priest from the full glory of the divine presence), and the blood of the sin offerings was sprinkled on and before the mercy seat (Leviticus 16:12-15). Jesus is our mercy seat, "whom God set forth as a **propitiation** [same word as mercy seat] by his blood, through faith" (Romans 3:25).

Cherubim are manifestations of God's glory. The cherubim woven into the covering of the tabernacle and the veil were reminders of the cherubim at the east of the Garden of Eden, which barred the way to the tree of life (Genesis 3:24). The two cherubim facing each other above the mercy seat represented the presence of God in the Holy of Holies.

Leading man towards God

Everything about the tabernacle was designed to lead man from the earthly to the heavenly – ascending, as it were, a scale of holiness:

* From the camp of Israel (1) into the outer court; (2) into the Holy Place; and finally (3) through the veil into the Holy of Holies.

* In the succession of metals: (1) bronze (the altar, laver and sockets in the outer court) is suggestive of mortal man; (2) silver (for the remaining sockets) hints at the coming Redeemer – the half-shekel redemption money provided the silver (see Exodus 30:11-16; 38:25-28); (3) gold (for the table

In a comprehensive study of the Cherubim and Seraphim, Brother Alfred Nicholls wrote the following:

"'The way into the holiest of all was not yet made manifest, while as the first tabernacle was yet standing' (Hebrews 9:8). But there was a way, for all that; and, significantly, it was both 'kept' by cherubim woven into the veil ... and the way also led to cherubim, golden ones which signified that the cherubic work was brought to its perfection." (*The Christadelphian*, 1973, page 10; series also published as an e-book) of showbread, lampstand, altar of incense, ark, mercy seat and cherubim) symbolises the divine.

- In the progression of colours woven into the linen: (1) scarlet, associated with humanity; (2) purple (a colour which combines red and blue), pointing to the priestly mediator; (3) blue, signifying the heavenly.

THE TABERNACLE – A PARABLE

The average Israelite would have only a vague idea of the significance of the tabernacle and all its parts. Yet to the spiritually discerning, and to us in retrospect, it was a living parable of the way by which man might one day come into God's holy presence. Everything about the tabernacle, and in particular the Holy of Holies, pointed to the Lord Jesus Christ. In almost every feature, it is Christ we see portrayed. He is the door, the altar of sacrifice, the laver of washing, the light of the lampstand; through him our prayers rise as incense to the Father; he is the bread of life; he is the veil (blue, purple and scarlet portraying his Godly, priestly, and human aspects; and the white linen his righteousness); he is the mercy seat – our meeting-place with God.

The Hebrew word most used for "tabernacle", *mishkan*, means 'dwelling-place', and the design speaks of a place fit for God's presence. The tabernacle was a place of meeting between man and God: "And there I will meet with you, and I will speak with you from above the mercy seat, from between the two cherubim which are on the ark of the Testimony" (Exodus 25:22); "I will dwell among the children of Israel and will be their God" (Exodus 29:45); "I will appear in the cloud above the mercy seat" (Leviticus 16:2).

In fact, the tabernacle could never truly be a **dwelling-place** for God: His ultimate purpose is to dwell with man in a spiritual sense: "I heard a loud voice from heaven saying, 'Behold the tabernacle of God is with men, and He will dwell with them, and they shall be His people. God Himself will be with them and be their God'" (Revelation 21:3). Meanwhile God dwells in those who make up His spiritual temple: "I dwell in the high and holy place, with him who has a contrite and humble spirit" (Isaiah 57:15). "You are the temple of the living God" (2 Corinthians 6:16; see also Ephesians 2:19-22).

"Gifts and sacrifices"

Now we need to return to the first verse of Hebrews 9: "Then indeed, even the first covenant had **ordinances of divine service** and the earthly sanctuary". We have concentrated so far on the "earthly sanctuary", the tabernacle, but we must also look at the *"ordinances of divine service"* – in other words what went on in the tabernacle. The daily, weekly, monthly and annual services consisted of *"gifts and sacrifices ... foods and drinks, various washings, and fleshly ordinances"* (9:9,10). These phrases summarise a multitude of offerings and rituals laid down in the Law of Moses, and carried out by the priests with the assistance of the Levites.

So does the writer to the Hebrews go through all those ordinances in detail to show how they were deficient? Does he examine one by one the sin offerings, burnt offerings and peace offerings, the fasts and feasts, to show how the sacrifice of the Lord Jesus Christ was better? No: he focuses almost exclusively on one event, one day in the annual cycle of offerings and feasts: the Day of Atonement. While *"the priests always went into the first part of the tabernacle* [the Holy Place], *performing the services"*, the High Priest went *"into the second part* [the Holy of Holies] *alone once a year, not without blood, which he offered for himself and for the people's sins committed in ignorance"* (9:6,7).

Reading those two verses quickly, we might think that on the Day of Atonement the ordinary priests were busy in the Holy Place while the High Priest was performing his tasks in the Holiest. Actually, on that Day, the Holy Place was empty: "There shall be no man in the tabernacle of meeting when [the high priest] goes in to make atonement in the Holy Place" (Leviticus 16:17). It was to be almost as if the Holy Place did not exist; as if the Law had been suspended – but of course that state of affairs did not last.

THE PROBLEM OF THE GOLDEN CENSER

Hebrews 9:3,4 seems at first sight to contain an error. From Exodus 30:1-10 it is clear that the incense altar was to be in the Holy Place, accessible every day and not just once a year. Yet Paul appears to include it with the furnishings of the *"Holiest of All, which had the golden censer and the ark of the covenant overlaid on all sides with gold"*. Has he made a mistake?

The incense altar itself was never in the Holiest. However, it is true that, on the Day of Atonement, a "golden **censer**" was (temporarily) in the Holiest. On that special day, the High Priest was instructed to fill this portable censer with coals of fire from the altar of incense. Then, "with his hands full of sweet incense beaten fine ... bring it inside the veil. And he shall put the incense on the fire [in the censer] ... that the cloud of incense may cover the mercy seat that is on the Testimony, lest he die" (Leviticus 16:12,13).

Having said that, the golden altar of incense was positioned **close to the veil** separating the Holy Place from the Holiest: "You shall put it **before the veil** that is before the ark of the Testimony" (Exodus 30:6). Interestingly, a similar detail appears in connection with the building of Solomon's temple: "Also the whole [incense] altar **that belonged to** the inner [holiest] sanctuary he overlaid with gold" (1 Kings 6:22, ESV).

What was actually achieved on the annual Day of Atonement? The High Priest entered briefly into the divine presence, but no other person could enter, *"the Holy Spirit indicating this, that the way into the Holiest of All was not yet made manifest while the first tabernacle was still standing"* (9:8). The tabernacle, though divinely ordained, was symbolic of the separation between man and his Maker. The people were cleansed, but only temporarily – it all had to be repeated the next year. And in any case sins were only **ritually** cleansed: what happened on that tenth day of the seventh month could never *"make him who performed the service perfect in regard to the conscience"* (9:9).

The faithful in Israel had long awaited the *"time of reformation"* (9:10), and at last Christ appeared *"as High Priest of the good things to come, with the greater and more perfect tabernacle not made with hands"* (9:11). The Lord Jesus has *"entered the Most Holy Place once for all, having obtained **eternal** redemption"* (9:12). And, unlike Aaron and his successors, our High Priest did not then have to step back into the Holy Place and carry on with the regular sacrifices, for *"when he had by himself purged our sins, [he] sat down at the right hand of the Majesty on high"* (1:3).

> "We heard him say, 'I will destroy this temple made with hands, and within three days I will build another made without hands'."   (Mark 14:58)

How was this redemption obtained?

"With his own blood"

"Without shedding of blood there is no remission" of sins (verse 22), and on the Day of Atonement no fewer than fifteen animals were offered. The sin offerings were a bullock for the High Priest and two goats for the people – one to be slain, and the other led away into the wilderness as the scapegoat. Then there were the burnt offerings

(see Leviticus 16; Numbers 29:7-11). Hebrews 9 does not list all these sacrifices. Nor does the writer go into every detail of the washings, sprinklings, and burning of incense, that took place on the Day of Atonement: he concentrates on the blood of the sin offerings.

No book of the New Testament mentions blood more frequently than Hebrews, and more than half of these references are in chapter 9. Jews were of course familiar with the shedding of the blood of animals, but the idea of sacrificial human blood was totally repugnant. Nevertheless, however uncomfortable Jewish readers might feel, Paul's argument must now lead to a discussion of the shedding of the blood of Christ: *"Christ came as High Priest ... not with the blood of goats and calves, but **with his own blood** he entered the Most Holy Place once for all, having obtained eternal redemption"* (9:11,12). On the Day of Atonement, the blood of the sin offerings had to be brought within the veil (Leviticus 16:14,15); the Lord Jesus, on the other hand, entered the Most Holy Place **with his own blood** to secure our redemption.

The words are startling! Paul's readers are asked to look at what happened on Calvary and see the dying Jesus not only as the High Priest but **also as the sacrifice**! At the Last Supper, Jesus said regarding the cup of wine, "This is **my blood** of the new covenant" (Matthew 26:28), so the idea of the shedding of Christ's blood as an atonement sacrifice should not have been strange to the Hebrews. At their baptism they

THE BLOOD OF CHRIST

The following are just a selection from many references:

- "This is my **blood** of the new covenant" (Matthew 26:28).

- "Having now been justified by his **blood** ..." (Romans 5:9).

- "The cup of blessing ... is it not the communion [fellowship, participation] of the **blood** of Christ?" (1 Corinthians 10:16).

- "The **blood** of Jesus Christ ... cleanses us from all sin" (1 John 1:7).

- "... who loved us and washed us from our sins in his own **blood**" (Revelation 1:5).

must have understood that Jesus died fulfilling all the types and shadows in the Law. Yet perhaps they still failed to appreciate that Jesus' blood truly was shed as an atonement sacrifice. The rest of chapter 9, and chapter 10, will explain more fully the wonder of Christ's work.

The red heifer

Verse 13 commences: *"For if the blood of bulls and goats ..."*, almost repeating what has gone before. But then something new is added: *"... and the ashes of a heifer, sprinkling the unclean ..."* This refers to a ritual that dealt with defilement associated with death, set out in Numbers 19. The sprinkled blood of a red heifer, and water purified by its ashes, provided the necessary cleansing. But why would Paul couple together "the blood of bulls and goats" with "the ashes of a heifer"? What the Day of Atonement and the ritual of the red heifer have in common is that they both deal with man's greatest enemy, death. They both have to do with salvation from sin and death.

There are, moreover, aspects of this ritual of the red heifer that place it **outside** the Law of Moses, foreshadowing the work of Jesus:

- It was enacted **later** than the Law given at Sinai – it looked to something beyond the Law;

- It took place outside the camp of Israel;

- Eleazar the son of Aaron, not Aaron himself, was charged with this observance – pointing to a future high priest;

- The person cleansed did not personally have to bring an offering;

- The ashes of one heifer (slain "once for all") provided a supply of purified water that could be used repeatedly; here is an example of a sacrifice that was effective to cleanse more than one person.

> The ashes of the heifer would contain 'activated charcoal', a form of carbon which is still used today in the purification of water.

Everything about this God-given ordinance pointed **beyond the Law** to another priesthood and another time – to the sacrifice of Christ that removed the defilement of death once for all. The fact that the cleansing ritual demanded the sprinkling of both blood and water again takes our minds to salvation through Jesus, who came "by water and blood" (1 John 5:6; cf. John 19:34). There are other details, too, that add to the significance of the ritual: the colour and condition of the heifer, the sprinkling of its blood seven times, the use of cedar wood, hyssop and scarlet thread: see Robert Roberts, *The Law of Moses*, chapter 28; W. F. Barling, *Law and Grace*, pages 182,183.

"How much more"

We were half way through a sentence which we must now complete! *"If the blood of bulls and goats*

> Though the writer to the Hebrews was doubtless inspired to make his own connection between the rituals of the Day of Atonement and the red heifer, they had in fact been brought together in a later Jewish practice that was not part of the original Law: the ashes of a red heifer were employed in the purification of the High Priest before the Day of Atonement.

"THROUGH [THE] ETERNAL SPIRIT"

What does this phrase mean? The law was bound by **time**; it was "symbolic for the present time"; the ordinances were "imposed until the time of reformation" (9:9,10). The offering and priesthood of Christ, on the other hand, had an **eternal** character, not limited by time – in fact, like the priesthood of Melchizedek, it was "according to the power of an **endless life**" (7:16). Jesus did not exist from eternity, but his character had an eternal quality, sinless and holy:

> "Jesus Christ [was] declared to be the Son of God with power **according to the spirit of holiness**, by the resurrection from the dead." (Romans 1:4)

and the ashes of a heifer, sprinkling the unclean, sanctifies for the purifying of the flesh, *how much more shall the blood of Christ*, who through the eternal Spirit offered himself without spot to God, cleanse your conscience from dead works to serve the living God?" (9:13,14). The Day of Atonement was the highest point of the Jewish calendar, the best that the Law could do in offering a remedy for sin; but all the High Priest could achieve on that day was **ritual** purification. Similarly, the sprinkling of a person with water from the ashes of a red heifer could offer no more than **ceremonial** cleansing. The shedding of the blood of the spotless Son of God, by contrast, is effective in cleansing the **conscience** of the believer.

"And for this reason ..." The writer is about to draw our attention to a momentous conclusion. Because the Lord Jesus entered "a greater and more perfect tabernacle"; and because he entered "not with the blood of goats and calves, but with his own blood", **for this reason** *"he is the Mediator of the new covenant, by means of death, for the redemption of the transgressions under the first covenant, that those who are called may receive the promise of the eternal inheritance"* (9:15).

From Hebrews 4:14 onwards, Paul has been demonstrating that the risen Lord Jesus Christ has become a High Priest greater than Aaron, a High Priest after the order of Melchizedek; now in chapter 9 he has shown that in Jesus we see not only **the High Priest**, but also **the sacrifice** by whose blood redemption was achieved, and finally **the Mediator** of the new covenant. At Sinai, Aaron was the High Priest, and Moses was the mediator. Jesus Christ is now "High Priest of the good things to come" (9:11), and he is **also** "the Mediator of the new covenant" – "a better covenant" (8:6). In him, the two functions become one.

The new covenant

Before we look at the next few verses, a comment must be made about the use of the words 'covenant' and 'testament' in different English translations. Both words are translations of the Greek word *diathēkē*, which is used throughout the New Testament and is the equivalent of the Old Testament Hebrew word for covenant, *berith*. The NKJV is more consistent than the KJV in translating *diathēkē* by 'covenant' – except in Hebrews 9:16,17, where the translators use "testament", evidently believing that the writer is referring to a will (today, we still refer to someone's 'last will and testament'). The Greek word **can** be used in connection with a human will, but here Paul must surely be writing in the context of Old Testament covenants – the very next verse takes us to the covenant made between God and Israel at Sinai. As for the word "testator", this suggests the covenant-victim or sacrifice by which a covenant is ratified. We shall therefore take the liberty of quoting the NKJV, replacing "testament" by "covenant", and "testator" by "covenant-sacrifice":

> *"For where there is a covenant, there must also of necessity be the death of the covenant-sacrifice. For a covenant is in force after men*

are dead, since it has no power at all while the covenant-sacrifice lives." (9:16,17)

The writer has already (7:22; 8:6-10) focused on the new covenant in Christ, a covenant that was better than the covenant at Sinai. Now, in 9:16-21, he takes his readers back to Sinai – to that great occasion when Israel entered into solemn covenant with their God (see Exodus 24). For all Jews, this most sacred occasion was the time when God bound Israel to Himself in an eternal covenant. Paul does not dispute this; in fact he rehearses in detail what took place at Sinai:

"Therefore not even the first covenant was dedicated without blood. For when Moses had spoken every precept to all the people according to the law, he took the blood of calves and goats, with water, scarlet wool, and hyssop, and sprinkled both the book itself and all the people, saying, 'This is the blood of the covenant which God has commanded you.' Then likewise he sprinkled with blood both the tabernacle and all the vessels of the ministry." (Hebrews 9:18-21; Exodus 24:1-8)

This description in verses 19 and 20 does not quite match the details in Exodus 24, which makes no mention of "goats", nor of "water, scarlet wool, and hyssop", but there is good evidence that all of these would have been involved – calves (bullocks or oxen) figured generally in burnt offerings; scarlet wool and hyssop would have been used to absorb and sprinkle the blood. Hebrews 9:19 mentions that Moses sprinkled the book of the law: in Exodus 24, this is not specifically stated, but from the fact that "Moses took the book of the covenant and read it in the hearing of the people" (verse 7) we can deduce that the book was indeed within reach of the sprinkled blood.

The Hebrews would certainly recognise everything that Paul said about those great events at Sinai. They would also recognise the brief description, in Hebrews 9:21, of the consecration with sprinkled blood of *"the tabernacle and all the vessels of the ministry"* (see Exodus 29:12; Leviticus 8:15). They would agree, moreover, that *"according to the law almost all things are purified with blood, and without shedding of blood there is no remission"* (verse 22).

"Copies of the things in the heavens"

Where, then, is Paul's argument leading? It is leading the Hebrews to the vital truth that the things that happened at Sinai, and in the consecration of the tabernacle, were but a shadow of better things to come; actually they were *"copies of the things in the heavens"* (9:23,24; compare 8:5); and the sacrifices and rituals of Sinai were sufficient for that purpose. *The heavenly things themselves"*, however, must be purified *"with better sacrifices than these"* (9:23). The Hebrews should no longer be in awe of Sinai and that ancient covenant, for it has been superseded by a more effective and lasting sacrifice, that of the sinless Son of God.

We are so used to speaking of 'The Old Testament' and 'The New Testament', that we may forget that "testament" means 'covenant'. Note the usage of "Old Testament" in 2 Corinthians 3:14.

EARLIER COVENANTS

The provision of skins from slain animals to cover the nakedness of Adam and Eve (Genesis 3:21) foreshadowed the principle of the shedding of blood in the ratification of a covenant. This was again the basis of God's covenant with Noah, who "took of every clean animal ... and offered burnt offerings on the altar" (Genesis 8:20). Abraham, in his turn, took sacrificial animals and cut them in two, and "there appeared a smoking oven and a burning torch that passed between those pieces. On the same day the LORD made a covenant with Abraham" (Genesis 15:9-18).

The remaining verses of chapter 9 spell out some of the ways in which the sacrifice of Christ excelled anything the law could offer:

- *"Christ has not entered the **holy places** [of the tabernacle or temple] **made with hands**, which are copies of the true, but into **heaven itself** ..."*
- *"not that he should offer himself **often** ... but now, **once** at the end of the ages ..."*
- *"the high priest enters the Most Holy Place every year with the **blood of another** [i.e., of animals] ... but ... [Jesus] has appeared to put away sin by the sacrifice of **himself**"* (9:24-26).

Chapter 10 will reinforce these comparisons between what the law failed to achieve, and what the Lord Jesus Christ has done. Meanwhile, chapter 9 concludes by making the point that *"it is appointed for men to die once, but after this the judgment"*. Men and women die and face judgment; Jesus, who shared our mortal nature, also died, *"to bear the sins of many"*; but *"to those who eagerly wait for him he will appear a second time, apart from sin, for salvation"* (9:27,28). The symmetry of these last two verses may be a little obscured, but the meaning is clear: the believer still faces **judgment**, but in Christ he is assured of **salvation**.

Did the Hebrews really want to continue year after year waiting with the throng in the temple court for a mortal high priest to emerge on the Day of Atonement? They have been called, rather, to join those who eagerly wait for Christ to return from God's right hand, glorious and immortal, for their salvation!

- "The goat [the live scapegoat] shall **bear** on itself all their iniquities ..." (Leviticus 16:22).
- "He **bore** the sin of many, and made intercession for the transgressors" (Isaiah 53:12).

POINTS TO PONDER

1. Why was it easier for Paul to talk about the tabernacle rather than the temple?

2. Imagine yourself as an Israelite approaching the Outer Court of the tabernacle. What can you actually see going on inside? Can you distinguish the priests from among the Levites? Would you recognise the High Priest?

3. What connection is there between the cherubim on the veil and the cherubim which God placed at the east of the Garden of Eden?

4. Read verse 15 slowly, 'unpack' it, and notice how well it summarises the work of God in Christ. In fact by simply rearranging the nouns we can spell out God's whole plan of redemption: transgression — death — redemption — mediator — covenant — promise — inheritance.

5. What sacrifices show that "without shedding of blood there is no remission" of sins?

Hebrews chapter 10

"A NEW AND LIVING WAY"

THE first half of chapter 10 summarises what has gone before, again driving home the contrast between the shadow and the substance, between the Law and Christ. Many words and phrases repeat what we have read earlier. Consider just verse 1 (set out below):

"For the law ...	"**For the law** made nothing perfect" (7:19); "**For the law** appoints as high priests men who have weakness" (7:28).
having a shadow ...	"priests ... according to the law ... serve the copy and **shadow** of the heavenly things" (8:4,5).
of the good things to come ...	"Christ came as High Priest of **the good things to come**" (9:11).
and not the very image of the things ...	"**the things in the heavens**" (9:23).
can never with these same sacrifices ...	"**gifts and sacrifices** are offered ..." (9:9).
which they offer continually year by year ...	"the high priest enters the Most Holy Place **every year**" (9:25).
make those who approach perfect ...	"... which cannot make **him who performed the service perfect**" (9:9).

Phrases in verses 2-4 similarly echo earlier statements. If the sacrifices under the law had been effective, *"would they not have ceased to be offered? For the worshippers, once purified, would have had no more consciousness of sins"* (10:2). Note, again, the distinction between ceremonial cleansing and purging of the **conscience** (see side panel).

THE BELIEVER'S CONSCIENCE

On four occasions in Hebrews, the writer emphasises how the sacrifice of Jesus was effective in purging the **conscience**:

1. "Sacrifices are offered which cannot make him who performed the service **perfect in regard to the conscience**" (9:9).
2. "How much more shall the blood of Christ ... **cleanse your conscience** ...?" (9:14).
3. "The worshippers ... would have had **no more consciousness** [same word] of sins" (10:2).
4. "Let us draw near ... having our hearts **sprinkled from an evil conscience**" (10:22).

An Israelite, reflecting on the Day of Atonement, might well go to his tent confident that his sins had been forgiven and forgotten. In fact, *"In those sacrifices there is a **reminder** of sins every year"* (10:3). The High Priest would have to undertake the same rituals the following year, and every year thereafter: *"For it is not possible that the blood of bulls and goats could take away sins"* (10:4, echoing 9:12,13,19).

"A body you have prepared"

Verses 5-10 take us to a psalm which reinforces the truth that sacrifices, in the end, were ineffective. Though divinely ordained, they could never truly give God pleasure:

> *"Therefore, when he came into the world, he said: 'Sacrifice and offering You did not desire, but a body You have prepared for me. In burnt offerings and sacrifices for sin You had no pleasure. Then I said, Behold, I have come – in the volume of the book it is written of me – to do Your will, O God'."* (10:5-7, quoting Psalm 40:6-8; cf. Isaiah 1:10-15; Hosea 6:6; Micah 6:6-8)

"In the volume of the book" surely refers to the countless ways in which the Hebrew scriptures foretold the coming of the Messiah, and how he would fulfil the Law and the Prophets. It was Jesus' delight to do his Father's will; and the Father took delight in the willing obedience of His Son: "I have come down from heaven, not to do my own will, but the will of Him who sent me ...

I always do those things that please Him" (John 6:38; 8:29). "Not my will, but Yours, be done" (Luke 22:42).

Offerings under the Law

Is it significant that in the quotation from Psalm 40 four descriptions of offerings are used: "sacrifice", "offering", "burnt offerings" and "sacrifices for sin"? In the psalm the four terms are different Hebrew words; and in Hebrews 10, separate Greek words are used. Between them, the four distinct words (whether in Hebrew or Greek) represent the four main groups of offerings under the Law:

1. "Sacrifice" has special reference to the peace offering;

2. "Offering" has special reference to the meal offering;

3. "Burnt offerings" are freewill offerings, wholly dedicated to the Lord;

4. "Sacrifices for sin" (which may here include trespass offerings) relate to specific sins.

The four terms thus cover the entire range of Levitical offerings, telling us that in giving his "body" – his life – Jesus made **every** offering and sacrifice redundant. The sacrifice of Christ fulfilled the **whole** Law. His sacrifice, moreover, was not the slaying of a dumb animal that was in no way associated with the one who offered; it was the voluntary laying down of the life of One made like those he came to save, One with whom sinners could feel connected.

"Has the LORD as great delight in burnt offerings and sacrifices, as in obeying the voice of the LORD? Behold, to obey is better than sacrifice, and to heed than the fat of rams."   (1 Samuel 15:22)

"Once for all"

In Jesus, laws and ordinances finally gave way to the offering of the Lamb of God who would voluntarily do God's will:

"He takes away the first that he may establish the second. By that will we have been sanctified through the offering of the body of Jesus Christ once for all." (10:9,10)

We have met the phrase "once for all" twice already:

- "Such a High Priest ... does not need daily, as those high priests, to offer up sacrifices ... for this he did **once for all** when he offered up himself" (7:26,27);

- "Christ came as High Priest ... not with the blood of goats and calves, but with his own blood he entered the Most Holy Place **once for all**, having obtained eternal redemption" (9:11,12).

In all three places where this phrase is used, two points are being made: that Jesus Christ our High Priest entered the Holiest (heaven itself) once for all; and the sacrifice he brought (himself) was a once-for-all offering.

In the next two verses of chapter 10, the point already made in 8:1 is repeated: whereas *"every priest **stands** ministering daily and offering repeatedly the same sacrifices ... this man, after he had offered one sacrifice for sins forever, **sat down** at the right hand of God"* (10:11,12). The Lord Jesus, having completed his Father's work,

could justifiably sit down. The risen Christ now waits, *"till his enemies are made his footstool"* (10:13, echoing 1:13 and Psalm 110:1).

"For by one offering he has perfected forever those who are being sanctified" (10:14). The law could "never with these same sacrifices ... make those who approach perfect" (10:1), but for those who have been "sanctified through the offering of the body of Jesus Christ once for all" (10:10), perfection is at last attainable. The words of Paul alongside may not have been written in the context of the Law, but how well they describe the perfection in Christ which was never attainable through the Law.

"MY EARS YOU HAVE OPENED"

The phrase in the Psalm, "my ears You have opened", is quoted in Hebrews as *"a body You have prepared for me"*, which is the way it reads in the Septuagint. At first sight, these phrases appear very different, but if we keep in mind the idea of a slave, the two versions can be reconciled. Under the Law, a servant who wished to offer lifelong service to a beloved master could have his ear pierced through ("opened") with an awl to the doorpost (Exodus 21:1-6). In New Testament times, a slave was a mere 'body' – and the alternative may have been more obvious to first century readers. As an obedient servant, the Lord Jesus willingly gave his body; his ears were opened; he sought always to do his Father's will: "Let this mind be in you which was also in Christ Jesus, who ... made himself of no reputation, taking the form of a bondservant, and coming in the likeness of men" (Philippians 2:5-7).

There is another way of understanding the "opened ear". Someone who is attentive to God's will is spoken of as having 'opened ears': "The Lord GOD ... awakens my ear to hear as the learned. The Lord GOD has opened my ear; and I was not rebellious" (Isaiah 50:4,5). In the case of Jesus, both interpretations are, of course, valid.

"When that which is perfect has come, then that which is in part will be done away." (1 Corinthians 13:10)

Chapter 8 drew attention to the "better covenant", as prophesied by Jeremiah; and now Jeremiah's words (31:33,34) are cited once more, demonstrating that *"the Holy Spirit also witnesses to us"* of the perfection that this better covenant would bring: *"Their sins and their lawless deeds I will remember no more"* (10:17).

"Now where there is remission of these [sins], *there is no longer* [any need for] *an offering for sin"* (10:18). This short verse summarises a long section of Hebrews, commencing as far back as chapter 3, on the superiority of the high priesthood and sacrifice of Christ. We have marvelled as the inspired writer, with incisive logic, has contrasted the "copy and shadow of heavenly things" (8:5) – the tabernacle, its priesthood and offerings – with the reality in Christ. The Lord Jesus has become High Priest for ever after the order of Melchizedek, a High Priest who entered the Holiest with his own blood, once for all.

"Boldness to enter the Holiest"

The author commences his next section with the astounding and humbling declaration that, because their Lord has entered the Holiest, **believers too** can enter the Holiest with him:

> *"Therefore brethren, having boldness to enter the Holiest by the blood of Jesus, by a new and living way which he consecrated for us, through the veil, that is, his flesh, and having a High Priest over the house of God, let us draw near with a true heart in full assurance of faith, having our hearts sprinkled from an evil conscience and our bodies washed with pure water."* (10:19-22)

This is the climax of a series of statements throughout the Epistle which describe the work of the Lord Jesus as the High Priest. Unlike the high priests under the Law, Jesus entered the Holiest once for all – for us:

- "Seeing then that we have **a great High Priest who has passed through the heavens** ... let us hold fast our confession. ... Let us therefore come boldly to the throne of grace ..." (4:14-16).

- "This hope we have as an anchor of the soul, both sure and steadfast, and which enters **the Presence behind the veil, where the forerunner has entered for us, even Jesus**" (6:19,20).

- "... into the second part [the Holy of Holies] the high priest went alone once a year, not without blood ... the Holy Spirit indicating this, that the way into the Holiest of All was not yet made manifest ... But **Christ** came as High Priest of the good things to come, with the greater and more perfect tabernacle ... **with his own blood he entered the Most Holy Place once for all**" (9:7-12).

- "**Christ has** not **entered** the holy places made with hands ... but **into heaven itself, now to appear in the presence of God for us** ... to put away sin by the sacrifice of himself" (9:24-26).

CHAPTER 13

In Christ Jesus "a new and living way" has been opened up so that **believers** can follow where their Lord has led: they too can enter the Holiest with their Lord. For an ordinary Jew, certainly for a Levite, even for a priest, this was unthinkable; he would have been awestruck by the thought. To enter the outer court was special; to enter the Holy Place was exclusively for the priests and Levites; while to step inside the Holy of Holies was the awesome privilege of the High Priest alone (in linen garments and enveloped in a cloud of incense), and then just once a year. Yet in Christ **we** can enter – with boldness! Through him we are reconciled with God; with the Lord Jesus as our intercessor we can enter the very presence of God in prayer.

"Through the veil"

Verses 20-22 contain some powerful phrases which deserve a closer look:

*   *"A new and living way"*: Back in chapter 9, it was noted that "the way into the Holiest of All was not yet made manifest while the first tabernacle was still standing" (9:8). There was no access into the Holy of Holies, no way into the presence of God. But through the death and resurrection of Jesus, a way – a way of life – has been opened.

*   *"Consecrated for us"*: We were reminded in chapter 9 that the first covenant was dedicated (consecrated) with blood (9:18). So, for us, a new covenant, and a new and living way, have been consecrated by the blood of Jesus.

*   *"Through the veil, that is, his flesh"*: The tabernacle veil was "woven of blue, purple, and scarlet thread, and fine woven linen ... woven with an artistic design of cherubim" (Exodus 26:31). Jesus himself is wonderfully portrayed in these features of the veil: he bore "the express image" (1:3) of the divine (blue); he partook of "flesh and blood" (2:14) (scarlet); in the purple we see his priestly and kingly roles combined. The cherubim barred the way to sinful mortals, but his righteousness (reflected in the fine linen, cf. Revelation 19:8) gave him access, entering "the Presence behind the veil" (6:19). Christ broke through the veil which separated the

The veil barring the way into the Holy of Holies

"I am the **way**, the truth, and the **life**. No one comes to the Father except through me."   (John 14:6)

Christ gave himself for the ecclesia "that he might sanctify and cleanse her with the washing of water by the word." (Ephesians 5:26)

"In Christ Jesus our Lord ... we have boldness and access with confidence through faith in him." (Ephesians 3:11,12)

Holy from the Most Holy – no wonder that, at his death, "the veil of the temple was torn in two from top to bottom" (Matthew 27:51).

• *"Our hearts sprinkled from an evil conscience and our bodies washed with pure water"*: We have already read of sprinkling in 9:13,19, but there may be an additional reference here to ceremonies to do with the consecration of the priests. Aaron and his sons were washed with water, and the anointing oil and blood were sprinkled on them (Leviticus 8:6,30). A spiritual sprinkling (by the blood of Christ) and washing (in baptism) is fitting, then, for those who would be part of a "royal priesthood" (1 Peter 2:9).

To have confidence and boldness is, essentially, to have faith. The Hebrews are exhorted to "draw near with a true heart in full assurance of **faith** ... for He who promised is **faithful**" (10:22,23).

GARMENTS WORN BY JESUS

In the Gospels we read of Jesus wearing garments of different colours. According to Luke, Herod with his men "arrayed Jesus in a gorgeous robe [*esthēs* apparel]" (23:11). The Greek word for "gorgeous" is *lampros*, also used of the "bright clothing" of the angel who appeared to Cornelius (Acts 10:30) – surely suggesting a **white** garment. In Matthew we read that when Pilate, in the next stage of the trial, delivered Jesus to be crucified, the soldiers "stripped him and put a **scarlet** robe [*chlamus*, cloak] on him" (27:28). John records (of the same occasion): "they put on him a **purple** robe [*himation*, outer garment]" (19:2). (The different words for the robes, and for the colours, indicate that two distinct garments are being referred to in the latter two references.) When the soldiers had mocked Jesus they "put his own clothes [*himatia*] on him" (Matthew 27:31); and "when they had crucified Jesus, [they] took his garments [*himatia*] and made four parts ... and also the tunic [*chitōn*, inner garment]. Now the tunic was without seam, woven from the top in one piece" (John 19:23). The description of Jesus' tunic takes us to the priestly ephod: "You shall make the robe of the ephod all of blue. There shall be an opening ... in the middle of it; it shall have a woven binding all around its opening" (Exodus 28:31,32). Here we have a strong suggestion that Jesus' tunic was **blue**; as a Jew, moreover, he would have had tassels of **blue** on the hem of his garment (Numbers 15:38).

It is surely no coincidence that the colours of the various garments connected with the life and death of Jesus correspond with those in the veil.

BOLDNESS AND CONFIDENCE

Several times in the Letter, the Hebrews are urged to have greater boldness (or confidence):

• "Whose house we are if we hold fast the confidence [*parrēsia*] ..." (3:6).

• "... if we hold the beginning of our confidence [*hypostasis*] steadfast to the end" (3:14).

• "Let us therefore come boldly [*parrēsia*] to the throne of grace ..." (4:16).

• "... having boldness [*parrēsia*] to enter the Holiest by the blood of Jesus" (10:19).

• "Therefore do not cast away your confidence [*parrēsia*] ..." (10:35).

• "So we may boldly [*tharreō*] say ..." (13:6).

"Full assurance of faith"

"Let us" recurs throughout Hebrews, always introducing an exhortation. Here we have three occurrences:

"Let us draw near with a true heart in full assurance of faith ... Let us hold fast the confession of our hope without wavering, for He who promised is faithful. And let us consider one another in order to stir up love and good works, not forsaking the assembling of ourselves together, as is the manner of some, but exhorting one another, and so much the more as you see the Day approaching." (10:22-25)

The word "faith" has already occurred a few times in earlier chapters, and so have the words "believe / belief / unbelief" which are from the same root:

- "So we see that they could not enter in because of **unbelief**" (3:19);
- "The word which they heard did not profit them, not being mixed with **faith** in those who heard it" (4:2);
- "We who have **believed** do enter that rest" (4:3);
- "... not laying again the foundation ... of **faith** toward God" (6:1);
- "... that you ... imitate those who through **faith** and patience inherit the promises" (6:12).

In Hebrews 10:22-25, the apostle encourages his readers to develop not just faith, but also hope and love:

"FAITH" IN OTHER EPISTLES

- "For in [the gospel] the righteousness of God is revealed from faith to faith; as it is written, 'The just shall live by faith'." (Romans 1:17).
- "Therefore we conclude that a man is justified by faith apart from the deeds of the law" (Romans 3:28).
- "The law is not of faith, but 'the man who does them shall live by them'." (Galatians 3:12).
- "Before faith came, we were kept under guard by the law, kept for the faith which would afterward be revealed. Therefore the law was our tutor to bring us to Christ, that we might be justified by faith. But after faith has come, we are no longer under a tutor" (Galatians 3:23-25).
- "... that I may gain Christ and be found in him, not having my own righteousness, which is from the law, but that which is through faith in Christ, the righteousness which is from God by faith" (Philippians 3:8,9).

"Let us draw near with a true heart in full assurance of **faith**";

"Let us hold fast the confession of our **hope** without wavering, for He who promised is faithful";

"Let us consider one another in order to stir up **love** and good works".

Other places where we find **Paul's triad of virtues** are listed on page 45.

Every brother and sister to whom Paul was writing had, at some time, come to the Gospel with a true heart, professing their faith in the Lord Jesus; they had given a good confession of their hope. It seems, however, that some no longer had that "full assurance"; they were not holding fast; they were "wavering"; their "good works" were not so obvious; some were even "forsaking the assembly". They needed to recover their earlier zeal, because the Day was fast approaching. **They needed to revive their faith!**

What "day" is being hinted at? As he wrote his Letter, Paul could no doubt see storm clouds on the horizon that heralded the overthrow of Jerusalem in AD 70. Some of his readers, however, may have been in denial, convinced that religious life in the city would continue undisturbed. They would have a rude awakening when that Day dawned. For every believer, there is a "day" to prepare for; all too soon, the day will dawn when it is too late – the day of our death may in any case be sooner than we think.

"Vengeance is mine"

The apostle's exhortations continue from verse 26 to the end of the chapter – and they include some severe warnings. The wavering Hebrews had to accept that if the "new and living way" in Christ was so much better, then the judgments for abandoning it were so much worse:

"If we sin wilfully ... there no longer remains a sacrifice for sins [repeating verse 18], *but a certain fearful expectation of judgment."* (10:26,27)

"Of how much worse punishment ... will he be thought worthy who has trampled the Son of God underfoot, counted the blood of the covenant by which he was sanctified a common thing, and insulted the Spirit of grace." (10:29)

"Vengeance is Mine, I will repay, says the Lord." (10:30, quoting Deuteronomy 32:35,36)

"It is a fearful thing to fall into the hands of the living God. And again, The Lord will judge His people." (10:31)

The reference to "the blood of the covenant" is interesting: Exodus 24 records how Moses "took the blood, sprinkled it on the people, and said, 'This is **the blood of the covenant** which the LORD has made with you'." At the same time the people vowed, "All that the LORD has said we will do, and be obedient" (24:8,7). Moses then ascended the mountain to receive from God the instructions regarding the tabernacle, and while he delayed the people corrupted themselves. When Moses came down from Mount Sinai, he found them worshipping a golden calf, playing and dancing (Exodus 32:1-20) – they had "counted the blood of the covenant a common thing"!

By not esteeming Christ as they should, were not the Hebrews at risk of showing contempt for his sacrifice?

"You have need of endurance"

In spite of the harsh warnings, the chapter finishes with a milder tone, as Paul invites the Hebrews to *"recall the former days in which ... you endured a great struggle* [athlēsis, as in an athletic contest, cf. 2 Timothy 2:5] *with*

The Law of Moses distinguished between unintentional and wilful sin:

"If a person sins unintentionally ... the priest shall ... make atonement for him; and it shall be forgiven him ... But the person who does anything presumptuously ... brings reproach on the LORD ... Because he has despised the word of the LORD, and has broken His commandment, that person shall be completely cut off; his guilt shall be upon him." (Numbers 15:22-31) *sufferings"*; and when they had been *"made a spectacle both by reproaches and tribulations"*. The writer himself acknowledges how they *"had compassion on me in my chains"*, and had *"joyfully accepted the plundering of your goods"* (10:32-34). Sadly, it seems as if some now lacked that earlier resilience, and perhaps also their former selflessness. Chapter 11 will remind them of great men and women of faith whose fortitude and courage never wavered.

In these concluding verses of chapter 10, Paul is not chiding the Hebrews, but in a fatherly way he is urging them to recover their earlier confidence in Christ. For those with faith and endurance, there is a reward: *"Therefore do not cast away your confidence, which has great reward. For you have need of endurance, so that after you have done the will of God, you may receive the promise"* (10:35,36).

CHRISTIANS AS A "SPECTACLE"

Persecuted Christians were being "made a spectacle"; they were being 'set on a stage' (the original Greek expression has given us the word 'theatre'). In his first letter to Corinth, Paul wrote: "I think that God has displayed us, the apostles, last, as men condemned to death; for we have been made a **spectacle** [theatre] to the world ..." (4:9).

THE SUFFERINGS OF THE JUDEAN ECCLESIAS

By an 'undesigned coincidence', Paul's first letter to the far-away ecclesia in Thessalonica provides evidence that the brothers and sisters in Jerusalem and Judea suffered for their faith in Christ: "For you, brethren [the Thessalonians], became imitators of the churches of God which are in Judea in Christ Jesus. For you also suffered the same things from your own countrymen, just as they did from the Judeans" (1 Thessalonians 2:14).

"The just shall live by faith"

The final quotation in this chapter starts with a phrase which literally means: 'Yet a very **very** little while' – Paul is emphasising what precious little time they have left! The phrase comes from Isaiah 26:20 and words from Habakkuk 2:3,4 then follow on. But whereas in Habakkuk it is "the vision" that will not tarry, in the Septuagint it is "the coming One" who will not tarry: *"For yet a little while, and He who is coming will come and will not tarry"* (Hebrews 10:37).

Meanwhile, however, just as the people of Habakkuk's day had faced the threat of a Chaldean invasion from the north, so just before AD 70 Jerusalem was facing destruction by the Romans. The Hebrews, as they listened to

> "A man is not justified by the works of the law but by faith in Jesus Christ ... if righteousness comes through the law, then Christ died in vain."   (Galatians 2:16,21)

Paul's message, should have understood how appropriate the quotation was for their situation. If the Hebrews would 'get the message', then they, like Habakkuk of old, would stand on the watchtower and faithfully prepare themselves: *"The just shall live by faith"* (10:38; also quoted in Romans 1:17; Galatians 3:11). If, on the other hand, *"anyone draws back, My soul* [says God] *has no pleasure in him".*

The writer adds his own personal encouragement, associating himself in the exhortation: *"But we are not of those who draw back to perdition* [or destruction], *but of those who believe* [have faith] *to the saving of the soul"* (10:39).

> "No one, having put his hand to the plow, and looking back, is fit for the kingdom of God."   (Luke 9:62)

POINTS TO PONDER

1. Look up "way" in a concordance: the number of occurrences is impressive! Find quotations where "way" refers to the 'way of life' which a believer should follow.

2. Many died in the wilderness when they were bitten by "fiery serpents". Moses was commanded to make a bronze serpent and put it on a pole, "and it shall be that everyone who is bitten, when he looks at it, shall live" (Numbers 21:4-9). No sacrifice was involved, so is not this an instance of 'living by faith'?

3. References to "faith" in Romans, Galatians and Philippians have been quoted. Look at the Letter of James and see how faith is contrasted with works in chapter 2.

4. How do we reconcile a God of love with a God of vengeance?

Hebrews chapter 11

"WITHOUT FAITH IT IS IMPOSSIBLE TO PLEASE HIM"

AT the end of chapter 10, the Hebrews were left with a choice: Were they among "those who draw back to perdition", or "those who have faith to the saving of the soul"? Moses had once confronted Israel with a similar choice: "I have set before you life and death, blessing and cursing; therefore choose life, that both you and your descendants may live" (Deuteronomy 30:19). Israel were often reluctant to choose life; they lacked faith and drew back. They were "a perverse generation, children in whom is no faith" (32:20). And even when they served God, it was by works, not faith – an attitude which persisted down to the time of Christ (and can still be displayed today!). "But the just shall live by his faith" (Habakkuk 2:4).

Occurrences of "faith"

How frequently does "faith" occur in the Old Testament? The answer is surprising: in the King James Version, only **twice** (in the verses from Deuteronomy 32 and Habakkuk 2 just quoted). Compare this with well over **two hundred** occurrences in the New Testament! "Faithful" and "faithfulness" do occur quite frequently in the Hebrew Scriptures, chiefly in relation to God's faithfulness; "truth" (from a related word) is again most often used to describe God's character.

The following are examples of the limited number of quotations which refer to the quality we are thinking of in the context of Hebrews 11:

- "My eyes shall be on the **faithful** of the land, that they may dwell with me; he who walks in a perfect way, he shall serve me" (Psalm 101:6).

- "May the LORD repay every man for his righteousness and his **faithfulness**" (1 Samuel 26:23).

Though the actual word "faith" may be rare, Hebrews 11 proves that this quality shone forth from the pages of the Old Testament in a number of exceptional individuals. Yet Hebrews 11 is not just a celebration of the nation's heroes. We miss the point of this great chapter if we do not realise that it is part of the argument Paul has been building up throughout the Letter. The lesson of chapter 11 is that it is only possible to please God by the way of faith; **and that way is outside the Law of Moses**. The faithful patriarchs of Israel did not even know the Law; and faithful characters who lived under the Law are cited in this chapter, not for their observance of the Law, but for other deeds of faith.

There is a parallel here with Stephen's speech, which has been touched on before.

"By [Jesus] everyone who **believes** is justified from all things from which you could not be justified by the law of Moses."   (Acts 13:39)

One of the underlying themes of Acts 7 is that God accepts the service of the faithful **wherever** they may be. Jews in the time of Jesus insisted that "Jerusalem is the place where one ought to worship" (John 4:20), whereas Stephen pointed out that the patriarchs, as well as their revered Moses, communed with God in places far from the Holy City and beyond the borders of the Land.

What is faith?

To the Hebrew mind, that question has to be answered in concrete terms, by reference to actual people. This, of course, will be done as the chapter proceeds. But first Paul prepares the ground by giving us an inspired definition or description of faith: *"Now faith is the substance of things hoped for, the evidence of things not seen"* (11:1).

"Substance" and "evidence" are the key words in this statement. In chapter 1, the word for "substance" (*hypostasis*) was translated "person" (1:3); there it conveys the idea of 'reality' or 'essence'. In 3:14, the same original word is translated "confidence". Here, in 11:1, it again means 'confidence' or 'assurance'. Wherever it is used, *hypostasis* suggests something with a foundation – the Greek word means literally a 'standing-under'.

"Evidence" (Greek, *elenchos*) has the sense of 'proof', 'conviction' or 'persuasion'. "Things hoped for" and "things not seen" are those things which God has revealed about Himself and His purpose, in which the believer places his total trust.

Faith is	
the assurance of	the conviction of
things hoped for	things not seen

The language of verse 1 is picked up at several places in the chapter (and a parallel passage from Corinthians is quoted alongside):

- "The **things which are seen** were not made of things which are visible" (verse 3).

- "Noah, being divinely warned of things **not yet seen** ..." (verse 7).

- "Abraham went out, **not knowing where he was going** ..." (verse 8).

- "These all died in faith, not having received the promises, but having **seen them afar off** ..." (verse 13).

- "By faith [Moses] ... forsook Egypt ... for he endured as **seeing Him who is invisible**" (verse 27).

"By [faith] *the elders obtained a good testimony"* (11:2). The word "elders" introduces the 'gallery of the faithful', the men and women about to be reviewed in this chapter. Being 'witnessed to', 'testified to', 'having obtained a good testimony', are expressions derived from

THINGS NOT SEEN

"We do not look at the things which are seen, but at the things which are not seen. For the things which are seen are temporal, but the things which are not seen are eternal ... For we walk by faith, not by sight."
(2 Corinthians 4:18; 5:7)

martur and *martureō* (from which we have the word 'martyr'), and which occur regularly in the New Testament – including the following places in Hebrews 11 and 12:

- "The elders **obtained a good testimony** [KJV, report]" (11:2; compare Acts 22:12; 1 Timothy 5:10).

- "Abel ... **obtained witness** that he was righteous, God **testifying** of his gifts" (11:4).

- "Enoch ... **had this testimony**, that he pleased God" (11:5).

- "And all these, **having obtained a good testimony** through faith" (11:39).

- "... we are surrounded by so great a cloud of **witnesses**" (12:1).

You might expect, after this introduction to the 'elders', that the chapter would now commence the review of the ancients of Israel, starting with Abel. First, however, we have verse 3, and for good reason: before looking at the worthies of old, the writer is inspired to consider faith in creation. It is as if, after penning verse 2, Paul turned to his Old Testament scriptures at Genesis 1 to pause at the creation record, moving on then to Genesis 4 (Abel), Genesis 6 (Noah), and so on.

Faith in God and creation

Belief in God is a matter of faith, as we shall see when we come to verse 6. Belief in creation, too, is a matter of faith: *"By faith we understand that the worlds were framed by the word of God, so that the things which are seen were not made of things which are visible"* (11:3). Some have argued that this verse is not about creation because the word used is not *kosmos* (the physical world) but *aiōnes* (the aeons or ages: the universe from the point of view of time and history). We note that *aiōnes* also occurs in chapter 1: "God ... has in these last days spoken to us by His Son ... through whom also He made the worlds [*aiōnes*]" (1:2).

> "The Son ... is the image of the invisible God, the firstborn over all creation. For by [RV, in] him all things were created that are in heaven and that are on earth, visible and invisible ... All things were created through him and for him."   (Colossians 1:15,16)

It is indeed true that God 'frames' (orders or controls) the 'ages' by His Word, intervening in the epochs of history to bring about His will. But this does not rule out an application of the statements in 1:2 and 11:3 to the **literal** creation. In any case, the statement "things which are seen were not made of things which are visible" has a more obvious application to the very beginning of time, when God's Word went forth to bring the universe into being. By faith we discern a purpose in creation **and** in all that has happened during the long ages of subsequent history. God's Word brought the universe into existence, and God's Word has gone forth "at various times and in various ways" (1:1) to fulfil His holy will.

The New Testament writers seem to use the Greek words *kosmos* and *aiōnes* to some extent interchangeably. Thus, in Acts 17:24, "God who made the **world** and everything in it", *kosmos* is used; but *kosmos* is also used in John 8:12, in "I am the light of the **world**". In fact, John, both in his Gospel and his epistles, almost always uses *kosmos*, and never *aiōn*, even in phrases like "My kingdom is not of this **world**" (John 18:36). We suggest it is unwise, therefore, to insist that "worlds" in Hebrews 11:3 (and 1:2) are **exclusively** the aeons of history.

If Hebrews 11:3 is solely about God's Word ordering the ages of history, then we would have to conclude that our 'chapter of faith' lacks any mention of faith in creation! The writer to the Hebrews knew that his readers then, and later readers like ourselves, needed a robust faith in creation, in order to resist the oppositions of the 'science' of the day.

"The elders"

The first of "the elders" to be mentioned is **ABEL** (Genesis 4:2-10). Both Cain and Abel brought an offering to God, but "righteous Abel" (Matthew 23:35) brought *"a more excellent sacrifice than Cain, through which he obtained witness that he was righteous"*. Many since "have gone in the way of Cain" (Jude 11) but the Seed-bearing line have sought, often imperfectly, to follow in the way of faithful Abel. He was the first of many to have his faith divinely attested: his blood "cried out from the ground" then (Genesis 4:10), and *"he being dead still speaks"* (11:4). Of course, his offering was not to be compared with that of the Seed himself, whose blood "speaks better things than that of Abel" (12:24).

ENOCH, "the seventh from Adam" (Jude :14), was faithful: *"By faith Enoch was taken away so that he did not see death, and was not found, because God had taken him ... he pleased God"* (11:5). The wording follows the Septuagint version of Genesis 5:24 – "Enoch was **well-pleasing to God**; and **was not found**, because God translated him". We learn from Jude that Enoch prophesied of the judgments that would come upon the wicked of his day for all their ungodly deeds. It would seem likely, then, that faithful Enoch was "taken away" for his own safety from the wrath of those – very likely including the vengeful Lamech (Genesis 4:23,24) – against whom he prophesied. Whereas Enoch was the seventh from Adam through Seth, Lamech was the seventh from Adam in the line of Cain.

Picking up on that last phrase, the writer pauses to consider what gives God pleasure: it is faith in His existence, and faith in the fact that He is a God who rewards those who trust in His promises: *"But without faith it is impossible* to please Him, for he who comes to God must believe that He is, and that He is a rewarder of those who diligently seek Him" (11:6). 'Coming to God' is one of the recurring themes of Hebrews, as the panel alongside proves.

"By faith NOAH ... prepared an ark ... condemned the world and became heir of the righteousness which is according to faith" (11:7). For Noah, the *"things not yet seen"* were the judgments which God was about to bring on a wicked world. *"Being divinely warned"*, he was *"moved with godly fear"* – fear in the sense of reverence for the Almighty. He had sufficient faith in God to build an ark far from the sea. He was concerned, moreover, not just *"for the saving of his household"*, but for those who, in unbelief, would perish in the Flood. This one verse about Noah is very compressed, but Peter adds detail, explaining how "the divine longsuffering waited in the days of Noah" (1 Peter 3:20); and "Noah, one of eight people, a preacher of righteousness" (2 Peter 2:5) was saved.

The lesson for the Hebrews was obvious: in faith, they should seek salvation in the 'ark' of Christ before their own world was swept away.

"By faith ABRAHAM obeyed when he was called to go out to the place which he would receive as an inheritance. And he went out, not knowing where he was going. By faith he dwelt in the land of promise as in a foreign country, dwelling in tents with Isaac and Jacob, the heirs with him of the same promise; for

he waited for the city which has foundations, whose builder and maker is God." (11:8-10)

In Abraham we see the greatest of the Old Testament men of faith. Abraham had faith in God's promises, and particularly those promises concerning a land (Genesis 13:14-17; 15:18-21; 17:8). He had faith in the promised inheritance, as did Isaac and Jacob, "the heirs with him of the same promise". Yet, at that time, God gave Abraham "no inheritance in it, not even enough to set his foot on" (Acts 7:5); Abraham "dwelt in the land of promise as in a foreign country". Hidden in those words was surely a call to the Hebrews to follow the example of Abraham. They, like all Jews, might boast of having

---

DIVINELY WARNED (GREEK, *CHRĒMATIZŌ*)

- "[Joseph and Mary], being divinely **warned** in a dream" (Matthew 2:12,22).

- "It had been **revealed** to Simeon ..." (Luke 2:26).

- "Cornelius ... was divinely **instructed** by a holy angel ..." (Acts 10:22).

- "Moses was divinely **instructed**" (Hebrews 8:5).

- "Noah, being divinely **warned** ..." (Hebrews 11:7).

COME TO ... APPROACH ... DRAW NEAR

- "Let us therefore **come** boldly **to** the throne of grace" (4:16).

- "He is also able to save ... those who **come to** God through him" (7:25).

- "The law ... can never ... make those **who approach** perfect" (10:1).

- "Let us **draw near** with a true heart" (10:22).

- "... for he who **comes to** God must believe" (11:6).

- "For you have not **come to** the mountain ... but you have **come to** Mount Zion" (12:18-22).

THOSE WHO 'CROSS OVER'

Hebrews are the descendants of Eber (Genesis 11:16-26), whose name is said to refer to those "beyond the river" or "those who have crossed over". Abraham crossed over from Mesopotamia, and true Hebrews down the ages have been those prepared to leave their country of origin and 'cross over'. Paul exhorts the Hebrews of his day to follow the example of Abraham the Hebrew and "go forth", for "here we have no continuing city" (13:13,14).

Abraham as their father (Matthew 3:9), but were they prepared to separate themselves from the apparent security of Jerusalem, as Abraham did from Ur, and go out into the unknown? Were they ready to consider themselves aliens "in a foreign country", as Abraham was? Were they, like Abraham, waiting "for the city which has foundations"?

The Hebrews seemed to be clutching on to a vain hope that the inheritance promised to Abraham and his descendants was through the Law. They had forgotten that the promises to the fathers were given long before the Law and were in no way dependent on the Law. Hebrews is not the only letter that teaches this:

- "For the promise that he would be the heir of the world was not to Abraham or to his seed through the law, but through the righteousness of faith ... He did not waver at the promise of God through unbelief, but was strengthened in faith ... And therefore 'it was accounted to him for righteousness'." (Romans 4:13-22).

- "Abraham 'believed God, and it was accounted to him for righteousness' ... So then those who are of faith are blessed with believing Abraham ... Christ has redeemed us from the curse of the law ... that the blessing of Abraham might come upon the Gentiles in Christ Jesus" (Galatians 3:6-14).

"By faith SARAH ... bore a child when she was past the age, because she judged Him faithful

who had promised" (11:11). Paul upholds Sarah's faith, and ignores the fact that both Sarah and Abraham laughed at the prospect of having a son in their old age (Genesis 17:17; 18:12). In Romans, too, it is their faith and not their doubt which is emphasised – see below. Sarah "judged Him faithful who had promised" and became the mother of a *"multitude – innumerable as the sand which is by the seashore"* (Hebrews 11:12). God seeks all who, in faith, judge Him to be faithful.

> "Not being weak in faith, [Abraham] did not consider his own body, already dead ... and the deadness of Sarah's womb. He did not waver at the promise ..."
> (Romans 4:19,20)

"These all died in faith"

Before continuing with the faith of Abraham, the writer reflects on the character and faith of the patriarchs, men (and women) of vision. Their qualities can be seen in the succession of powerful verbs in these four verses: *"These all died ... not having received ... seen afar off ... assured ... embraced ... confessed ... declare plainly ... seek ... desire"* (11:13-16). Like Abraham himself, they *"confessed that they were strangers and pilgrims on the earth"* (cf. Genesis 23:4; Leviticus 25:23; 1 Peter 2:11); *"they seek a homeland"*; *"they desire a better, that is, a heavenly country. Therefore God is not ashamed* to be called their God, for He has prepared a city for them".

The Hebrews should have noticed a very pointed lesson in verse 15: *"If [the patriarchs] had called to mind that country from which they had come out, they would have had opportunity to return."* Abraham and his family went out and did not look back; they had no nostalgia for the things they had left behind. Why were the Hebrews so reluctant to follow suit?

"By faith Abraham, when he was tested, offered up Isaac" (11:17). Abraham's greatest test of faith came when *"he who had received the promises offered up his only begotten son, of whom it was said, 'In Isaac your seed shall be called'"*. At God's command, the patriarch set off with his son: "the two of them went together". When Isaac asked, "Where is the lamb for a burnt offering?" Abraham replied, "My son, God will provide for Himself the lamb" (Genesis 22:1-8). Abraham was ready to obey God's instructions, but as he was about to slay his son his hand was stayed; he had proved his faith in God and belief in resurrection from the dead, *"from which he also received* [Isaac] *in a figurative sense"*. What happened there on Mount Moriah foreshadowed in poignant detail the sacrifice of the Lamb of God, which the divine hand did not prevent. And Jesus rose from the dead, not in a figure but in glorious reality.

The line of faith continues: **ISAAC** and **JACOB** shared Abraham's faith, and (as with Abraham) the writer does not dwell on attempts to bring about the will of God in their own way, but on the moments when in faith they allowed God's way to prevail. So Hebrews passes over the deceit of Jacob in obtaining Esau's blessing and looks rather to the eventual outcome, when *"Isaac blessed Jacob **and** Esau concerning things to come"* (11:20). For Esau the things to come were temporary material blessings – "the fatness of the earth, and of the dew of heaven from above" (Genesis 27:39); while for Jacob, Isaac reserved the eternal covenant blessings: "May God Almighty bless you ... multiply you ... give you the blessing of Abraham ... that you may inherit the land ..." (28:3,4).

A clash of wills arose when Jacob came to bless Joseph's sons, Manasseh (the firstborn) and Ephraim. To Joseph's displeasure, Jacob crossed his hands to bestow the greater blessing on Ephraim (Genesis 48:8-20). The act of faith that is emphasised in Hebrews, however, is that *"Jacob, when he was dying, blessed **each** of the sons of Joseph"* (11:21), reflecting the double blessing and God's purpose that **two** tribes should come out of Joseph.

Jacob's eyes had become "dim with age, so that he could not see" but with the eye of faith he could assure Joseph: "God will be with you and bring you back to the land of your fathers" (Genesis 48:10,21). With this vision in mind, Jacob made Joseph swear to him that he would not be buried in Egypt but with his fathers (Genesis 47:29-31). Incidentally, where Genesis

"Was not Abraham our father justified by works when he offered Isaac his son on the altar? ... Abraham believed God, and it was accounted to him for righteousness." (James 2:21-23)

The Hebrew words for "bed" and "staff" have the same consonants but can be translated differently according to the vowels that are inserted. The Septuagint translators chose to render the word in Genesis 47:31 as "staff".

records that "Israel bowed himself on the head of the bed", Hebrews 11:21 tells us that Jacob *"worshipped, leaning on the top of his staff"*.

"By faith JOSEPH … made mention of [called to mind, as in verse 15] *the departure* [exodus] *of the children of Israel, and gave instruction also concerning his bones"* (11:22). Many other happenings could have been chosen to illustrate Joseph's faith, but the writer focuses on Joseph's far-sighted vision of the day when God would fulfil the promise to Jacob: "I will go down with you to Egypt, and I will also surely bring you up again" (Genesis 46:4; cf. 15:16). Joseph demonstrated the faith of his ancestors: he believed the promises; his hope was bound up in an inheritance, not in Egypt but in the promised land. When he gave instruction concerning his bones (50:24,25; Exodus 13:19; Joshua 24:32) he was surely looking towards the day when he would be reunited with his fathers through resurrection.

"By faith Moses"

Amram and Jochebed are not mentioned by name, but it is **their** faith that is highlighted first. Pharaoh had commanded that all Hebrew baby boys were to be killed, but *"By faith MOSES, when he was born, was hidden three months by his parents, because they saw he was a beautiful child; and they were not afraid of the king's command"* (11:23). It may be that Moses' parents were given angelic guidance concerning their son, but it required faith to commit Moses to the bulrushes and trust in providence.

Once again, there are parallels here with Stephen's speech, but whereas Stephen goes into more detail about Moses' dealings with his fellow-Israelites (both in Egypt and later in the wilderness), Hebrews concentrates rather on his spiritual vision. In a crescendo of short dynamic phrases (11:24-29), a picture is built up of a man with his gaze fixed on the infinite – concerned not with the temporal but with the eternal:

- He *"refused to be called the son of Pharaoh's daughter"*;
- *"choosing rather to suffer affliction … than to enjoy the passing pleasures of sin"*;
- *"esteeming the reproach of Christ greater riches than the treasures in Egypt"*;
- *"he forsook Egypt, not fearing the wrath of the king"*;
- *"he endured as seeing Him who is invisible"*;
- *"he kept the Passover and the sprinkling of blood"*;
- *"they passed through the Red Sea as by dry land"* (11:24-29).

Just as the faith of the patriarchs was captured earlier in a succession of verbs – "seen", "embraced", "confessed" etc. – so the faith of Moses, his unswerving resolve to look higher and farther, is caught in these expressions.

For a lesser man, life in the court of Pharaoh would have been attractive, but Moses chose rather to serve God in the wilderness and suffer affliction with his people. Of course, Moses could not have foreseen all the challenges that lay ahead; there would be occasions when he was tested to the limit: "I am not able to bear all these people alone, because the burden is too heavy for me" (Numbers 11:14). Yet he stood the strain and his faith faltered only in the matter of speaking to the rock when the people cried for water (Numbers 20:7-12). "You did not **believe** Me [said God] ... therefore you shall not bring this assembly into the land which I have given them".

Moses *"esteemed the reproach of Christ greater riches than the treasures in Egypt"* (11:26). In bearing reproach he was a type of the Son of God of whom the Psalmist wrote: "For Your sake I have borne reproach ... reproach has broken my heart" (Psalm 69:7,20).

> "Let us go forth to [Jesus], outside the camp, bearing his reproach."
>
> (Hebrews 13:13)

"He looked to the reward" – a phrase which takes us back to verse 6: "God is a rewarder of those who diligently seek Him". The word "reward" (in the KJV, "recompense of reward") occurs in Hebrews 2:2; 10:35 and here in 11:26.

"He endured as seeing Him who is invisible" (11:27). Of all the men of faith, Moses was the one who had the greatest claim to have seen God. It is true, of course, that "no one has seen

God at any time" (John 1:18; 1 Timothy 6:16), yet Moses saw a manifestation of God at the burning bush: he had "turned aside to look ... Moses hid his face, for he was afraid to look upon God" (Exodus 3:4-6). Moreover, God spoke to Moses "face to face" at Sinai; and Moses caught a glimpse of God's glory "in the cleft of the rock" (Exodus 33:11,22,23). Yet the statement in 11:27 is not only about a passing glimpse of God's glory but about Moses' recognition in faith that God, though invisible, was powerful to lead His people out of Egypt and into the promised land.

"By faith he kept the Passover and the sprinkling of blood, lest he who destroyed the firstborn should touch them" (11:28). Nine plagues had come on Egypt, and still Pharaoh had not let Israel go. Moses and Aaron were now to instruct every household among the Israelites to take a lamb without blemish, and strike (sprinkle) its blood on the doorposts and lintel, so that "when He sees the blood on the lintel and on the two doorposts, the LORD will pass over the door and not allow the destroyer to come into your houses" (Exodus 12:23).

To their credit, the children of Israel did as they were instructed and prepared in faith for the great journey. As soon as they became aware of the Egyptians pursuing them, however, "they were very afraid, and ... cried out to the LORD". Moses nonetheless held his nerve and said to the people: "Stand still, and see the salvation of the LORD" (Exodus 14:10,13). Yet again, Israel's moment of doubt is overlooked in Paul's

"OUR PASSOVER"

"... Christ Jesus, whom God set forth as a propitiation by his blood, through faith ... because in His forbearance God had **passed over** the sins that were previously committed." (Romans 3:24,25)

"For indeed Christ, our **Passover**, was sacrificed for us."

(1 Corinthians 5:7)

> "All our fathers were under the cloud, all passed through the sea, all were baptized into Moses in the cloud and in the sea, all ate the same spiritual food, and all drank the same spiritual drink. For they drank of that spiritual Rock that followed them, and that Rock was Christ."   (1 Corinthians 10:1-4)

review of events, and the section concludes on a positive note. "Tell the children of Israel to **go forward**" (verse 15), was God's instruction. So, *"By faith they passed through the Red Sea as by dry land, whereas the Egyptians, attempting to do so, were drowned"* (11:29).

The Hebrews must ponder their own situation: the Lamb of God had died; Christ, their Passover, had been sacrificed; they had been saved from death – yet they were still fixated on the past, apparently doubting the salvation that was theirs in Christ. They revered Moses for the Law that bore his name; it was time now to follow his example of faith and go forward.

Joshua and the Judges

We move on quickly from the Red Sea to Jericho. If we again compare Hebrews 11 with Acts 7, we see that Stephen has much more to say about happenings during the 40 years wilderness wanderings. It is not that the author of Hebrews could find no deeds of faith in that period: he could have cited the faithful spies, Caleb and Joshua; he could have mentioned more examples of the faith of Moses. But Hebrews 11 is not a full recital of every act of faith; rather, a careful selection of occasions when men and women made a stand against particular challenges: when they drew back from temptation, and went forth in faith.

JOSHUA is not mentioned by name, but it was by his courage and faith that Jericho was

conquered: *"By faith the walls of Jericho fell down after they were encircled for seven days"* (11:30). Joshua exhibited faith, and so did the people. Imagine their initial disbelief that a city could be overcome, not by men of war, but by priests bearing the ark and blowing trumpets – and, on the seventh day, a final shout (Joshua 6:1-16)! Surely the exhortation for Israel, and now for the Hebrews, was that foes are conquered in God's strength and not man's.

> "For the weapons of our warfare are not carnal but mighty in God for pulling down strongholds."   (2 Corinthians 10:4)

*"By faith the harlot **RAHAB** did not perish with those who did not believe, when she had received the spies with peace"* (11:31). Rahab knew that Jericho was "doomed to destruction" (Joshua 2:9; 6:17) but in faith – Joshua having promised to save her and her household – she went forth from the city before it was burned with fire: "And the young men who had been spies went in and brought out Rahab ... and all that she had ... **outside the camp** of Israel" (Joshua 6:23). Could there have been a more dramatic object lesson for those now being urged to go "outside the camp"? By marrying into the royal tribe, moreover, Rahab became an ancestor of Messiah (Matthew 1:5). Her scarlet cord hinted at the means by which her greater Son, through the shedding of his blood, would redeem the faithful.

> "Was not Rahab the harlot also justified by works when she received the messengers and sent them out another way?"
>
> (James 2:25)

*"And what more shall I say? For the time would fail me to tell of **GIDEON** and **BARAK** and **SAMSON** and **JEPHTHAH** ..."* (11:32). Curiously, the historical order of names in each of the pairs is reversed. The exploits of Deborah and Barak against the Canaanites, celebrated in a victory song, confirmed their faithful commitment to God (Judges 4 & 5). Gideon needed reassurance in the signs of the fleece, but in the final conflict with Midian his faith was vindicated: the battle was won by a mere three hundred men (Judges 6 & 7). Jephthah was driven out of his father's house without an inheritance; but in faith, having delivered the Ammonites, he carried out the solemn vow concerning his daughter (Judges 11). Samson (Judges 13-16) achieved renown for rash and daring ventures, not all of which we would associate with a man of God; yet he was one of those who "out of weakness were made strong". In his last extremity he called in faith upon his God and brought down a pagan temple upon the lords of the Philistines.

"Of David and Samuel and the prophets"

SAMUEL, of course, comes before David: a man of fierce loyalty to God, as shown in his

displeasure that Israel should want a king (1 Samuel 8). He died in faith, having anointed David as successor to Saul. Samuel was the last of the judges but also the first of the great prophets (see Acts 3:24). God gave His own testimony regarding the stature of Samuel: "Even if Moses and Samuel stood before Me, My mind would not be favourable toward this people" (Jeremiah 15:1).

DAVID was one who *"through faith subdued kingdoms"* and *"obtained promises"* (11:33). In faith he prepared for the building of the temple, confident that Solomon would fulfil his ambitions. David's faith failed him in time of temptation, yet it was in faith that he could write: "Blessed is he whose transgression is forgiven, whose sin is covered" (Psalm 32:1).

Finally, in this impressive 'roll-call of the faithful', the writer adds **THE PROPHETS**. They may not be named, but some can be identified by their experiences (11:33-38): a divine hand *"stopped the mouths of lions"* to save Daniel (Daniel 6) and *"quenched the violence of fire"* to save Shadrach, Meshach and Abed-Nego (Daniel 3). Hezekiah, encouraged by Isaiah and aided by the angel of the Lord, *"turned to flight the armies of the* [Assyrians]" (2 Kings 19; Isaiah 37). The widow of Zarephath and the Shunammite *"received their dead* [sons] *raised to life again"* by Elijah and Elisha, respectively (1 Kings 17:17-24; 2 Kings 4:8-37) – and Paul may even have had in mind the widow of Nain's son, or Lazarus, raised by Jesus.

When we come to *"mockings and scourgings ... chains and imprisonment ... [those who were] destitute, afflicted, tormented"*, we think of Job (Job 1,2), Joseph (Genesis 39:20), Jeremiah (chapters 37,38); in New Testament times, Stephen (Acts 7:58,59), James and Peter (Acts 12:1-4), and Paul himself (2 Corinthians 11:23-27). And did not the Master himself suffer these things, and more? Of all men and women of faith it can truly be said, *"of whom the world was not worthy"*.

> "My brethren, take the prophets, who spoke in the name of the Lord, as an example of suffering and patience."
> (James 5:10; cf. Matthew 5:11,12)

"They wandered about in sheepskins and goatskins ... in deserts and mountains, in dens and caves of the earth." This would certainly apply to Elijah (2 Kings 1:8), and again to John the Baptist (Matthew 3:4), and many others who were hounded for their faith, outcasts from society. Were the Hebrews asking themselves where **they** stood? Were **they** prepared to be "strangers and pilgrims on the earth" (11:13)?

The heroes of faith, *"having obtained a good testimony through faith, did not receive the promise"*; they endured *"that they might obtain a better resurrection"*. They await their reward, *"God having provided something better for us,*

that they should not be made perfect apart from us" (11:35-40).

Hebrews 11 is sometimes viewed as an isolated chapter, not really connected to the argument of the Letter as a whole. This is far from the case: the writer is telling his readers that their salvation is not to be found in the familiar comfortable environment in which they have been brought up, in the apparent security of the temple and its worship. They have to "go out" like Abraham, to "suffer affliction with the people of God" like Moses, to be prepared, if necessary, for exile "in dens and caves of the earth". The Hebrews faced an uncertain future and needed the faith and fortitude of those remarkable characters who had gone before.

POINTS TO PONDER

1. Explain why Cain's offering was not acceptable.

2. According to Hebrews 11:6 God is "a rewarder" (see also 10:35; 11:26 and Matthew 6:1-6). Should the prospect of a reward be our reason for serving God?

3. Describe how Abraham's journey with Isaac to Moriah pointed forward to the sacrifice of Jesus in Jerusalem.

4. Hebrews 11 is all about the **actions** of men and women of faith. Trace the sequence of verbs in this chapter which reveal what they **did**, e.g., "offered, "prepared", "obeyed" ...

5. What other faithful characters in the Old Testament could well have been included in Hebrews 11, but are not mentioned?

Hebrews chapter 12

"LOOKING UNTO JESUS"

THE procession of faithful men and women did not end with Hebrews 11. There is one more name to be added to the roll of the faithful, to the "cloud of witnesses", and it is that of **JESUS**.

Thus *"surrounded by so great a cloud of witnesses"*, including the Lord Jesus, those to whom the apostle wrote must be zealous to follow their example. It was not good enough to boast, "Abraham is our father", or "We are Moses' disciples" (John 8:39; 9:28); ancestry of itself is of no account. God demanded of them (and demands of us) the same intense effort as was shown by the faithful of old: *"Let us lay aside every weight, and the sin which so easily ensnares us, and let us run with endurance the race that is set before us"* (12:1).

"A cloud of witnesses"

The language of verses 1 & 2 is that of the Greek Games, which Paul alludes to in several of his letters (see panel). The saints to whom he writes, having shed "every weight" and encumbrance, are ready to run their race "with endurance". The "cloud of witnesses" are those who have run the race before, seated in ranks around the track, and from whom the runners draw inspiration. Jesus himself is, as it were, the judge or umpire;

WEIGHTS AND BURDENS

In referring to "every weight" which the Hebrews were to lay aside, was Paul thinking of (among other things) the burden of the Law of Moses which they were slow to cast off? Peter, addressing the Jerusalem Council, acknowledged that the Law was a burden: "Now therefore, why do you test God by putting a yoke on the neck of the disciples which neither our fathers nor we were able to bear?" (Acts 15:10,28; see also Matthew 23:4).

ATHLETIC METAPHORS

- "Do you not know that those who run in a race all run, but one receives the prize? ... And everyone who competes for the prize is temperate in all things. Now they do it to obtain a perishable crown, but we for an imperishable crown ... I discipline my body and bring it into subjection, lest, when I have preached to others, I myself should become disqualified." (1 Corinthians 9:24-27)

- "Reaching forward to those things which are ahead, I press toward the goal for the prize." (Philippians 3:13,14)

- "I have fought the good fight, I have finished the race, I have kept the faith. Finally, there is laid up for me the crown of righteousness." (2 Timothy 4:7,8)

"He is the head of the body ... the beginning, the firstborn from the dead, that in all things he may have the preeminence."

(Colossians 1:18)

"These things says the Amen, the Faithful and True Witness, the Beginning of the creation of God."

(Revelation 3:14)

"I am the Alpha and the Omega, the Beginning and the End, the First and the Last." (Revelation 22:13)

he is elevated in a seat of honour and the runners are *"looking* [up, or away] *unto Jesus"*, the greatest inspiration of all. What powerful imagery!

We wonder whether the phrase *"author and finisher of our faith"* (12:2) continues the athletic metaphor: is the writer referring to the fact that the Lord Jesus Christ is there at the start and finish of our race of discipleship? There are positive hints earlier in the Letter that this is so: the word here translated "author" is translated "captain" in chapter 2 – Jesus is "the captain of their salvation" (2:10); while in chapter 6 he is referred to as our "forerunner" (6:20). Certainly, the risen Christ is with us in the race for life: "He who has **begun** a good work in you will **complete** it until the day of Jesus Christ" (Philippians 1:6). In the side panel are other verses which are surely relevant.

"For the joy that was set before him [he] *endured the cross, despising the shame."* We may still be in athletic imagery, for a runner fixes his gaze on the finishing post and the wreath (*stephanos*) that awaits the winner. (Of course, in the race of discipleship, not just one but **all** are winners, by grace, if they run faithfully.) Those who ran in the Grecian Games were the celebrities of their day; Jesus, by contrast, had to "endure the cross" and "did not hide [his] face from shame and spitting" (Isaiah 50:6). But the humiliation of the cross ultimately led on to glory: "Therefore God also has highly exalted him and given him the name which is above every name"

(Philippians 2:9). The Lord Jesus *"has sat down at the right hand of the throne of God"* – words once more echoing Psalm 110.

While enduring the agony and shame of crucifixion, our Lord looked to the "joy that was set before him". The words of the psalm will have sustained him: "I have set the LORD always before me ... Therefore my heart is glad, and my glory rejoices; my flesh also will rest in hope ... In Your presence is fulness of joy; at Your right hand are pleasures forevermore" (Psalm 16:8-11).

"Consider him"

The whole purpose of writing to the Hebrews was to encourage them to "consider Jesus". The next few verses suggest that they may have become discouraged, possibly resentful of the sufferings they were having to endure. So Paul directs their attention first of all to the sufferings of the Lord himself: *"Consider him who endured such hostility from sinners against himself, lest you become weary and discouraged in your souls"* (12:3). Their afflictions did not compare with those of Jesus in Gethsemane or on Calvary.

"Let us not grow weary while doing good, for in due season we shall reap if we do not lose heart." (Galatians 6:9)

Unlike Jesus, they had *"not yet resisted to bloodshed, striving against sin"* (12:4) – but within a very short time, there **would** be bloodshed in Jerusalem. They must become resilient, ready for whatever lay ahead. They must acknowledge the need for discipline, spoken of here as "chastening" (12:5,6, quoting Proverbs 3:11,12). Actually, if they were suffering, then it was evidence that the Father was truly calling them to be sons: *"My son, do not despise the chastening of the Lord ... If you endure chastening, God deals with you as with sons ... Human fathers ... chastened us as seemed best for them, but He for our profit, that we may be partakers of His holiness"* (12:5-10; quoting Deuteronomy 8:5). Discipline may seem *"painful"* but it *"yields the peaceable fruit of righteousness to those who have been trained by it"* (12:11). *"Therefore strengthen the hands which hang down, and the feeble knees, and make straight paths for your feet, so that what is lame may not be dislocated, but rather be healed"*; they are to *"pursue peace ... and holiness"* (12:12-14).

Do these verses suggest that the Hebrews had lost momentum; that some had deviated from the path; that there was perhaps discord in the ecclesia (or their section of it)? They needed to take swift action, *"looking carefully lest anyone fall short of the grace of God"*.

They were to watch out, *"lest any root of bitterness springing up cause trouble"*. The case of Esau is cited: a *"profane person ... who for one morsel of food sold his birthright"* (12:15-16). Esau is not among the men of faith in chapter 11. His mind was set on earthly things, and

though *"he wanted to inherit the blessing"*, it was (as we saw in connection with 11:20) material blessing, not the patriarchal covenant blessing, that really interested him. Esau *"found no place for repentance, though he sought it diligently with tears"* – this could suggest that he could find 'no way to change Isaac's mind', but equally 'no way to change his own mind'.

> "I make this covenant [said Moses] ... that there may not be among you a root bearing bitterness or wormwood ..."
> (Deuteronomy 29:14,18)

If the Hebrews could read between the lines, they would have perceived an exhortation directed at **them**, not to risk losing their Christian 'birthright' for the sake of temporary material gain!

Two mountains

Paul is coming towards the end of his Letter. He will conclude in chapter 13 with brotherly appeals and kindly exhortations, but first of all, in the remainder of chapter 12, he is inspired to take his readers back once more to Sinai and draw lessons from Israel in the wilderness.

We are given vivid descriptions of two mountains: Mount Sinai and Mount Zion. For the Jew who loved the Law, there was nothing negative about Mount Sinai, for that was where

> "Strengthen the weak hands, and make firm the feeble knees. Say to those who are fearful-hearted, Be strong, do not fear!" (Isaiah 35:3,4)
>
> "Depart from evil and do good; seek peace and pursue it."
> (Psalm 34:14)

> "Now Mount Sinai was completely in smoke, because the LORD descended upon it in fire ... the whole mountain quaked greatly ... the trumpet sounded long and became louder and louder."
> (Exodus 19:18)
>
> "You came near and stood at the foot of the mountain, and the mountain burned with fire ... with darkness, cloud, and thick darkness." (Deuteronomy 4:11)

Moses "received the living oracles to give to us" (Acts 7:38). It was at Sinai that Israel entered into a covenant with their God, to be "a special people ... a kingdom of priests and a holy nation" (Exodus 19:5,6). Yet the Law, though God-given, proved in the end to be "the ministry of death ... the ministry of condemnation" (2 Corinthians 3:7-9).

In fact, Moses had received the Law in circumstances which caused fear among the people of Israel. Paul's question to the Hebrews was therefore: Why would they want to persist in observing the Law of Sinai from which they had been redeemed? *"For you have not come to the mountain that may be touched* [that is, touched on pain of death] *and that burned with fire, and to blackness and darkness and tempest, and the sound of a trumpet and the voice of words, so that those who heard it begged that the word should not be spoken to them anymore ... And so terrifying was the sight that Moses said, 'I am exceedingly afraid and trembling'"* (12:18-21).

This was not the mountain to which their faith in Christ had brought them. Rather:

> *"You have come to Mount Zion and to the city of the living God, the heavenly Jerusalem, to an innumerable company of angels, to the general assembly and church of the firstborn ... to God the judge of all, to the spirits of just men made perfect, to Jesus the Mediator of the new covenant, and to the blood of sprinkling that speaks better things than that of Abel."* (12:22-24)

What a contrast! They had probably never thought of the Law being associated with terror; nor perhaps had they thought of the hope of the Gospel in terms of the heavenly Jerusalem. The blessings which the Lord Jesus Christ had brought them were unspeakably better than those under the Law. They were now associated with:

- *"Mount Zion and the city of the living God, the heavenly Jerusalem"* – not the Jerusalem they knew, but "the city which has foundations", "the New Jerusalem ... descending out of heaven from God" (Revelation 3:12; 21:10). God has been referred to three times already in Hebrews as "the living God" (3:12; 9:14; 10:31) and in Him they should place their confidence.

- *"an innumerable company of angels"* – "Those who are counted worthy to attain that age ... are equal to the angels" (Luke 20:35,36).

- *"the general assembly* [or, festal gathering] *and ecclesia of the firstborn who are registered in heaven"* – "Israel is My Son, My firstborn" (Exodus 4:22) but through unbelief that generation of firstborns died in the wilderness. The saints in Christ are "predestined to be conformed to the image

> "The LORD will record, when He registers the peoples: 'This one was born there' [in Zion]." (Psalm 87:6)

of His Son, that he might be the firstborn among many brethren" (Romans 8:29). "Rejoice because your names are written in heaven" (Luke 10:20).

- *"God the judge of all"* – "The LORD will judge His people" (Deuteronomy 32:36; Hebrews 10:30).

- *"the spirits of just men made perfect"* – The saints who come to Zion are those who "are not in the flesh but in the Spirit" (Romans 8:9). They have been justified by grace (not Law), and made perfect in Christ.

- *"Jesus the Mediator of the new covenant"* – The contrast is with Moses the mediator of the old covenant. Jesus is "Mediator of a better covenant, which was established on better promises" (8:6; 9:15).

- *"the blood of sprinkling that speaks better things than that of Abel"* – Abel's blood "cried out" (Genesis 4:10); his death foreshadowed the One whose blood would "speak better things" and bring redemption. The sprinkling of the blood at Sinai had no lasting effect, but the elect in Christ are promised salvation by the "sprinkling of the blood of Jesus Christ" (1 Peter 1:2).

"Do not refuse him who speaks"

Though Christian believers were not, like Israel, trembling and afraid at the foot of Mount Sinai, and though they had been reconciled to God by the death of His Son, they should still realise that one day they must face "God the judge of all". In earlier chapters the apostle has already tried to alert his readers to the seriousness of their situation. Looking back over those warnings we notice especially words like "neglect", "depart", "disobey", "fall away", "sin wilfully":

- "If the word spoken through angels [that is, the Law at Sinai] proved steadfast ... how shall we escape if we neglect so great a salvation [in Christ] ..."? (2:2,3).

- "Beware, brethren, lest there be in any of you [as there was in Israel in the wilderness] an evil heart of unbelief in departing from the living God" (3:12).

- "For who, having heard, rebelled? ... with whom was He angry forty years? ... to whom did He swear that they would not enter His rest, but to those who did not obey?" (3:16-18).

- "For the word of God is living and powerful, and sharper than any two-edged sword ... all things are naked and open to the eyes of Him to whom we must give account" (4:12,13).

- "It is impossible for those who were once enlightened ... if they shall fall away, to renew them again to repentance, since they crucify again for themselves the Son of God" (6:4-6).

- "If we sin wilfully after we have received the knowledge of the truth, there no longer remains a sacrifice for sins, but a certain fearful expectation of judgment, and fiery

SINAI AND ZION IN GALATIANS

The problems affecting the Galatians and the Hebrews were different, and yet there were certain similarities. The Galatians were turning again "to the weak and beggarly elements" of the Law (Galatians 4:9); the Hebrews' problem was that they had not fully moved on from the Law. It is not too surprising, then, to find in both letters an allegory contrasting Sinai and Zion – representing the old and new covenants.

Paul challenged the Galatians with a beautifully crafted allegory contrasting Hagar and Sarah, Ishmael and Isaac, Sinai and Jerusalem: "For these are the two covenants: the one from Mount Sinai which gives birth to bondage, which is Hagar – for this Hagar is Mount Sinai in Arabia, and corresponds to Jerusalem which now is, and is in bondage with her children – but the Jerusalem above is free, which is the mother of us all" (4:24-26). The allegory in Hebrews 12:18-24 is simpler but no less powerful, contrasting the Mount Sinai of the Law and the heavenly Jerusalem to which we belong in Christ.

> "Take heed to yourselves, lest you forget the covenant of the LORD your God which He made with you ... For the LORD your God is a consuming fire, a jealous God."
> (Deuteronomy 4:23,24; see also Exodus 24:17)

indignation which will devour the adversaries ... It is a fearful thing to fall into the hands of the living God" (10:26-31).

Paul does not spare them! Note how the warnings get steadily more severe as the Letter progresses, and the warning at the end of chapter 12 is the severest of all: *"See that you do not refuse Him who speaks. For if they did not escape who refused Him who spoke on earth, much more shall we not escape if we turn away from Him who speaks from heaven ... For our God is a consuming fire"* (12:25,29).

"A kingdom which cannot be shaken"

Between verses 25 and 29 is Haggai's prophecy of a great shaking yet to come upon the earth. At Sinai, the voice of the Almighty *"shook the earth"* and frightened the people of Israel, *"but now He has promised, saying, 'Yet once more I shake not only the earth, but also heaven'. Now this, 'Yet once more', indicates the removal of those things that are being shaken ... that the things which cannot be shaken may remain"* (12:26,27 quoting Haggai 2:6).

The message is terrifyingly clear: those who refuse to listen to God's voice through His Son will hear His voice of judgment; they will be shaken. But there is a better way: *"Since we are receiving a kingdom which cannot be shaken, let us have grace, by which we may serve God acceptably with reverence and godly fear"* (12:28).

> "There is a river whose streams shall make glad the city of God ... God is in the midst of her, she shall not be moved."
> (Psalm 46:4,5)

The world around the believers would be shaken: what was important was that their faith should remain unshakeable – that, like the Colossians (1:23), they should "continue in the faith, grounded and steadfast ... not moved away from the hope of the gospel which you heard".

POINTS TO PONDER

1. What "weights" must the disciple lay aside?

2. Why was the giving of the Law associated with "blackness and darkness and tempest"?

3. Trace the idea of God's called-out ones being "the firstborn".

4. What other prophecies, besides Haggai, refer to latter-day earthquakes?

Hebrews chapter 13

"LET US GO FORTH TO HIM, OUTSIDE THE CAMP"

H EBREWS is a Letter in which exhortation follows exposition, and chapter 13 continues the same pattern. From the dramatic scenes of Sinai and Zion, Paul turns once more to words of encouragement. In fact, because of the chapter division, we hardly notice how abruptly the mood switches from "Our God is a consuming fire" at the end of chapter 12, to "Let brotherly love continue" at the start of chapter 13!

Lessons and warnings continue (13:1-9); there is a brilliant piece of reasoning from the Law (13:10-12); and the epistle concludes with Paul's final, heartfelt, appeal to his uncertain readers to "go forth to Jesus, outside the camp, bearing his reproach".

The practical exhortations cover a range of pastoral topics:

- Brotherly love
- Entertaining strangers
- Remembering prisoners and those mistreated
- Marriage
- Covetousness
- Obeying ecclesial elders
- Countering strange doctrines
- Going forth "outside the camp"

- Offering God praise and thanks
- Doing good and sharing
- Praying
- Bearing with the word of exhortation

Do these exhortations reflect what Paul knew of the Hebrews themselves? Of course, all ecclesias need to be exhorted on these topics but perhaps the Hebrews needed help on particular issues. Possibly, as a result of their concentration on the Law and the temple, they were overlooking some of the basic demands of ecclesial life and fellowship.

Good works

Earlier in the Letter, Paul had commended them for their "work and labour of love which you have shown toward his name, in that you have ministered to the saints, and do minister" (6:10). That might have been some time before, and maybe their good works had lapsed. They should be ready, once again, to *"entertain strangers, for by so doing some have unwittingly entertained angels"* (13:2). Remember Abraham (Genesis 18) and Lot (Genesis 19)!

In chapter 10 he had asked them to "recall the former days in which ... you were made a spectacle both by reproaches and tribulations ... became

> "For this you know, that no fornicator ... has any inheritance in the kingdom of Christ and God."
> (Ephesians 5:5)

companions of those who were so treated; for you had compass on on me in my chains, and joyfully accepted the plundering of your goods ..." (10:32-34). It had been natural in those former days to *"remember the prisoners"* (13:3), and they should now continue to do so. *"Marriage is honourable among all, and the bed undefiled"* (13:4) could suggest that there had been reports of infidelity, and they are warned that *"God will judge"*. They must recover Christ-like virtues.

To add that their *"conduct be without covetousness"* (13:5) does not necessarily mean that covetousness was a problem – though it may have been. If they had left the priesthood, they would very likely have been poor, and would also be suffering from loss of esteem. But where was their confidence in God and the fellowship of His Son? Verse 5 quotes words by which God had reassured Jacob (Genesis 28:15), Joshua (1:5) and Solomon (1 Chronicles 28:20): *"He Himself has said, 'I will never leave you nor forsake you.' So we may boldly say: 'The Lord is my helper; I will not fear. What can man do to me?'"* (13:5,6, quoting Deuteronomy 31:6; Psalm 118:6, LXX). It was a time for unwavering trust in God.

Remember your rulers

A special concern for Paul was the attitude of his readers to their elders: three times in this final chapter he refers to *"those who rule over you"* (verses 7,17,24), and in a way that suggests there could be some tension between the group to which he was writing and their ecclesial elders:

> "You also be patient. **Establish your hearts**, for the coming of the Lord is at hand." (James 5:8)

"Remember those who rule over you, who have spoken the word of God to you, whose faith follow, considering the outcome of their conduct" (13:7). Why would they not respect their elders? These, after all, had included apostles who received the Gospel from the Lord Jesus himself (2:3). The Hebrews were privileged to have had them as teachers; they should show them proper esteem and follow their faith. The phrase, "considering the outcome of their conduct", suggests that some may have been martyred.

The Hebrews could have felt unsettled as a result of the fate of these apostles and elders in Jerusalem. They needed stability – to *"be established"* (verse 9). Is it against this background, then, that we should look at verse 8, which otherwise seems slightly unconnected with what has gone before – *"Jesus Christ is the same yesterday, today, and forever"* (13:8)? It is a statement that gives reassurance. Whatever traumas the ecclesia had gone through, the Lord Jesus was still there. In everything he had done, was now doing, and would continue to do, he was the same – constant and unchanging; he is their High Priest for ever. A similar assurance of continuity was given in chapter 1: "To the Son he says ... You, Lord, in the beginning laid the foundation of the earth ... They will perish, but you remain ... they will be changed. But **you are the same**, and your years will not fail" (1:10-12, quoting Psalm 102:25-27).

But it is not just Jesus who remains the same. "Jesus Christ the same yesterday, today, and forever" (the "is" has been added in translation) is also a statement that the **Gospel** remains the same; it is the same Gospel that was preached to Abraham (Galatians 3:8), and has been proclaimed unchanged throughout the ages. The constancy of the divine word takes us back to the opening words of the Letter: "God, who **at various times and in various ways** spoke in time past ... has **in these last days** spoken to us by His Son" (1:1,2).

Verse 8 leads on, in turn, to the warning in verse 9: *"Do not be carried about with various and strange doctrines."* The Gospel cannot change, so they must not be carried away by "another Gospel" (cf. Galatians 1:6,7). Nothing should distract them from the Gospel of grace: *"For it is good that the heart be established by grace, not with foods which have not profited those who have been occupied with them"* (13:9). Many of them had partaken of the "foods" of the sacrifices, but to no lasting profit. There was no reason to be obsessed any longer with "foods and drinks, various washings, and fleshly ordinances imposed until the time of reformation" (9:10).

> "You are not under law but under grace."
> (Romans 6:14)

Throughout the Letter, the apostle has tried to educate his readers in the grace of God through Jesus Christ:

- "... that he, by the **grace** of God, might taste death for everyone" (2:9).

- "Let us therefore come boldly to the throne of **grace** ... find **grace** to help in time of need" (4:16).

- "Of how much worse punishment ... will he be thought worthy ... who has insulted the Spirit of **grace**?" (10:29).

- "Looking carefully lest anyone fall short of the **grace** of God" (12:15).

- "... receiving a kingdom which cannot be shaken, let us have **grace**" (12:28).

"We have an altar"

Under the Law of Moses, the priests were allowed to eat parts of certain sacrifices, and the eating of such a meal was symbolic of fellowship with God (see 1 Corinthians 9:13, quoted below). That was considered a great privilege (a 'perk' of the job).

> "Do you not know that those who minister the holy things eat of the things of the temple, and those who serve at the altar partake of the offerings of the altar?"
> (1 Corinthians 9:13)

Some of the Hebrews to whom Paul wrote had been priests. Remember that very significant statement in Acts: "A great many of the **priests** were obedient to the faith" (Acts 6:7). Were those former priests feeling deprived of the satisfaction of service at the altar, including the partaking of sacrificial meals? Having chosen to serve the Lord Jesus Christ, were they now missing their former duties n the temple?

Paul argues that in Christ they are no longer serving the altars of the Law; they have another 'altar' – a new and better way of approach to God through the sacrifice of His Son. Verse 10 puts this cryptically: *"We have an altar from which those who serve the tabernacle have no right to eat"* (13:10). The context is the law concerning sin offerings (Leviticus 4) and in particular the sin offerings which the High Priest brought on the Day of Atonement (Leviticus 16). The lesson of verse 10 is that on the very day of the year when the Aaronic High Priest came closest to God by entering the Holy of Holies he was still forbidden from enjoying a symbolic meal with God: he had *"no right to eat"*. The Law did not give man true fellowship with God!

There were sin offerings of which the priests **could** eat (Leviticus 6:26) but the sin offerings on the Day of Atonement were among those that could **not** be eaten (Leviticus 6:30). On that Day a bull and one of the two goats (the other was the scapegoat) were slain, and their blood was brought into the Holiest, but significantly the flesh and carcases were burned outside the camp (Leviticus 16:27): *"For the bodies of those animals whose blood is brought into the sanctuary by the high priest for sin, are burned [consumed by burning, not burned sacrificially] outside the camp ..."* (13:11). All was burned, including the portion that (in another situation) might have been for the priests.

Everything about the Day of Atonement pointed forward to Christ. In what happened at Calvary we see the connection (and contrast) between the sin offerings burned **"without the camp"** on the Day of Atonement, and the Lord's once-for-all offering for sin – **"outside the gate"**. *"Therefore Jesus also, that he might sanctify the people with his own blood, suffered outside the gate"* (13:12). His death was outside the temple, outside Moses' Law; he died as an outcast (as it were) from the congregation of unbelieving Israel.

The clear implication for followers of Jesus is that they too were now outcasts – there was nothing more to hold them in the temple and its services. In fact, if the Hebrews continued to associate themselves with temple worship in Jerusalem, they would cut themselves off from Christ.

"Therefore let us go forth to him ..."

This, then, is the writer's last passionate plea to the waverers: a final challenge to those still hankering after Moses, and the heritage of Moses' Law. This section of chapter 13 is very much aimed at them: in fact, one would need to be a priest (or someone very well educated in the Law) to appreciate the points Paul is making.

The exhortation of verse 13 then follows on seamlessly: *"Therefore let us go forth to him, outside the camp bearing his reproach."* They were not called upon to give their lives but they must be prepared to leave behind the things

"Would [Aaron and his sons] ever have wondered why the flesh of the bullock that was offered on behalf of the sins of the nation was burned outside the camp, and no portion was available for them to eat? Israel was being taught in a graphic fashion that the law could only bring men and women as far as the altar. It revealed sin as the great adversary of mankind, and showed how sins must be forgiven if men and women are to draw close to God" (Michael Ashton, *The Beauty of Holiness*, page 40).

they cherished. They no longer belonged to the priesthood and the temple that were so soon to pass away.

"For here we have no continuing city, but we seek the one to come. Therefore by him let us continually offer the sacrifice of praise to God, that is, the fruit of our lips, giving thanks to his name" (13:14,15). The sacrifices will soon cease; the temple will be destroyed; their beloved city will shortly be no more. For those who have followed Christ Jesus outside the camp there are, however, sacrifices they can bring: their total devotion, their "sacrifice of praise" – the fruit of lips giving thanks to God's name.

> "O Israel, return to the LORD your God ... Say to Him, 'Take away all iniquity; receive us graciously, for we will offer the sacrifices of our lips'." (Hosea 14:2)

And a vital part of the disciple's sacrifice is in service to his fellow-pilgrims: *"Do not forget to do good and to share, for with such sacrifices God is well pleased"* (13:16). And, again, their elders should not be overlooked: *"Obey those who rule over you, and be submissive, for they watch out for your souls, as those who must give account. Let them do so with joy and not with grief, for that would be unprofitable for you"* (13:17).

Having himself nurtured new communities of believers, and feeling a "deep concern for

all the ecclesias" (2 Corinthians 11:28), Paul knew all about the burdens carried by ecclesial elders, and would regularly be asked for advice in difficult situations. In the present situation he would want to help everyone in the ecclesia, including the elders (who doubtless, at some stage, would have seen this Letter).

"Pray for us"

These final exhortations are a call to be more outward-looking. Brothers and sisters, now as well as then, have a tendency to be self-centred. How regularly do **we** stop and pray for those who guide our ecclesias, and the affairs of the Brotherhood? Think of those who spend long hours applying scriptural wisdom to ecclesial problems, who take decisions on preaching work, or the organisation of care facilities: *"Pray for us; for we are confident that we have a good conscience, in all things desiring to live honourably. But I especially urge you to do this, that I may be restored to you the sooner"* (13:18,19). Thirty or more years previously, Paul had been viewed with deep suspicion by the Jerusalem ecclesia. By now, he hopes, they can trust his sincerity. Even more important, however, is that they accept his appeals to them on behalf of Christ.

The last title of the Lord Jesus to be used in this Letter is *"that great Shepherd of the sheep"* (13:20). This should have stirred thoughts of the "Shepherd of Israel ... You who dwell between the cherubim" (Psalm 80:1); but also, surely, of

> "We urge you, brethren, to recognise those who labour among you, and are over you in the Lord and admonish you, and to esteem them very highly in love for their work's sake."
> (1 Thessalonians 5:12,13)

> "Finally, brethren, pray for us ... You yourselves know how you ought to follow us, for we were not disorderly among you ... but worked with labour and toil night and day."
> (2 Thessalonians 3:1,7,8)

> "Shepherd the flock of God which is among you ... being examples to the flock; and when the Chief Shepherd appears, you will receive the crown of glory that does not fade away." (1 Peter 5:2-4)

the One who declared himself to be "the good shepherd" (John 10:11). The words should, moreover, have stirred the conscience of those who did not appear to be giving their own shepherds the esteem they deserved.

The phrase *"the blood of the everlasting covenant"* summarises, in a way, all that the writer has expounded and explained about God's work in His Son. The blood of Christ embraces all that the Father undertook from Eden onwards, to prepare the world for the sacrifice of the Redeemer. Blood takes us to Moriah, to Sinai, to Golgotha; the blood of Christ is the focus of our own weekly re-enactment of that solemn feast in the Upper Room. This "blood of the new covenant" binds the saints in fellowship with their Lord.

So Paul prays, finally, for his readers, that *"the God of peace ... make you complete in every good work to do His will, working in you what is well pleasing in His sight, through Jesus Christ, to whom be glory forever and ever. Amen"* (13:20,21).

> "Now the God of peace be with you all. Amen." (Romans 15:33)

Would the Hebrews have the wisdom and humility to heed Paul's appeals? *"I appeal to you, brethren, bear with the word of exhortation, for I have written to you in few words"* (13:22).

We cannot believe that these "few words" were without effect and we trust that spiritual lives were saved by this searching Letter.

The release of Timothy will have been welcome news (13:23). The writer (whose identity, of course, they knew) hoped to come with him shortly. Who knows if Paul wrote a separate letter to the Jerusalem elders? But he encourages his readers to *"greet all those who rule over you, and all the saints"* (13:24). *"Those from Italy* [very likely, believers from Italy residing in the town from which Paul was writing] *greet you"* (13:24).

"Grace be with you all. Amen." (13:25)

POINTS TO PONDER

1. What "various and strange doctrines" could divert us from the true Gospel now?

2. In what ways may we have to bear the reproach of Christ?

3. Do we "forget to do good and to share"?

Epilogue

HOW did the Hebrews react to Paul's Letter? If (as in chapter 6) he was "confident of better things of you, yes, things that accompany salvation", then we can hope that they severed, once and for all, those lingering ties that bound them to the things of Moses, and embraced wholeheartedly their calling in Christ.

Can we imagine Paul's own feelings as he waited to hear how his Letter had been received? There could have been similarities with the occasion when he anxiously awaited the Corinthians' response to one of his letters, and was greatly relieved "by the coming of Titus ... when he told us of your earnest desire, your mourning, your zeal for me, so that I rejoiced even more" (2 Corinthians 7:7). It seems likely that the Letter to the Hebrews would soon be followed up by personal contact, for Paul urges them to *"pray for us ... especially ... that I may be restored to you the sooner"* (13:19). We can only speculate about such a meeting and what might have been discussed.

And what about "those who rule over you", whom Paul was equally trying to help? If Paul's appeals were heeded, then surely the elders will have communicated their gratitude to the apostle. We trust that a more united Jerusalem ecclesia prospered ... at least until they were overtaken by the calamities of AD 70.

Further reading

MANY commentaries and background sources were consulted during the preparation of this Study Guide, and the following is a short-list of those particularly recommended for further reading:

Christadelphian works:

- Robert Roberts, *The Law of Moses*, Birmingham, 1898.
- John Carter, *The Letter to the Hebrews*, CMPA, 1947.
- John Martin, *Hebrews: Study Notes*, CSSS, 1976.
- Michael Ashton, *Tabernacle Study Guide*, CMPA, 1989.

- Kathleen & Leen Ritmeyer, *The Ritual of the Temple in the Time of Christ*, Carta, 2002.
- W. F. Barling, *Law and Grace*, CMPA, 1952; *Hebrews: A Thematic Study*, CMPA, 2012.

Non-Christadelphian works:

- W. Kay, *The Speaker's Commentary: Hebrews* [especially the Introduction], John Murray, 1881.
- A. Edersheim, *The Temple, Its Ministry & Services at the Time of Jesus Christ*, The Religious Tract Society, 1874.